D0205892

'Race', Gender and the Education of Teachers

OPEN UNIVERSITY PRESS
Gender and Education Series
Editors
ROSEMARY DEEM
Professor of Educational Research, University of Lancaster
GABY WEINER
Professor of Education at South Bank University

TITLES IN THE SERIES

Managing Women
Sue Adler, Jenny Laney and Mary Packer

Boys Don't Cry
Sue Askew and Carol Ross

Science and Technology in the Early Years
Naima Browne (ed.)

Untying the Apron Strings
Naima Browne and Pauline France (eds)

Changing Perspectives on Gender
Helen Burchell and Val Millman (eds)

Co-education Reconsidered
Rosemary Deem (ed.)

Girls and Sexuality
Lesley Holly (ed.)

Women in Educational Management
Jenny Ozga

A History of Women's Education in England
June Purvis

Shaping Up to Womanhood
Sheila Scraton

'Race', Gender and the Education of Teachers
Iram Siraj-Blatchford (ed.)

Whatever Happens to Little Women?
Christine Skelton (ed.)

Dolls and Dungarees
Eva Tutchell (ed.)

Just a Bunch of Girls
Gaby Weiner (ed.)

Women and Training
Ann Wickham

'Race', Gender and the Education of Teachers

Edited by Iram Siraj-Blatchford

Open University Press
Buckingham • *Philadelphia*

Open University Press
Celtic Court
22 Ballmoor
Buckingham
MK18 1XW

and
1900 Frost Road, Suite 101
Bristol, PA 19007, USA

First Published 1993

A catalogue record of this book is available from the British Library.

ISBN 0 335 19017 0 (pb)

Library of Congress Cataloging-in-Publication Data
'Race', gender and the education of teachers/Iram Siraj-Blatchford
  (ed.).
    p. cm. — (Gender and education series)
Includes bibliographical references and index.
ISBN 0-335-19017-0
1. Teachers — Training of — Great Britain.   2. Women teachers —
  Training of — Great Britain. 3. Discrimination in higher
  education — Great Britain. 4. Sex discrimination in higher
  education — Great Britain. 5. Educational equalization —
  Great Britain.   I. Siraj-Blatchford, Iram.   II. Series.
LB1725.G6R33   1993
370.71'0941 — dc20   92-29884
                                                          CIP

Typeset by Colset Pte Ltd, Singapore
Printed in Great Britain by J.W. Arrowsmith Ltd, Bristol

Contents

List of Contributors

Maud Blair is a lecturer in the School of Education in the Open University. Before that she worked as an advisory teacher for multi-cultural education in Cambridgeshire. She has taught in schools in Zimbabwe and in England and also worked as a youth development officer and a community researcher in Cambridge.

Pam Boulton is head of the Centre for Cross-Curricular Issues in the School of Education at Sheffield Hallam University. Much of her work is in the secondary sector of initial teacher education. She has an interest in student-centred learning in schools and higher education. She has a daughter and a son.

Leone Burton is professor of Education (Mathematics and Science) at the University of Birmingham. Her publications include *Thinking Things Through* (Simon & Schuster) and *Girls Into Mathematics Can Go* (Cassell), the first book in the UK to address gender and mathematics teaching. More recently she has become interested in the implications for equal opportunities of adopting different management styles in higher education.

Lynda Carr is director of the Equal Opportunities Commission's Employment Department, having headed its Education Department for the previous ten years. She managed the EOC's formal investigation into initial teacher education in 1989 and was UK co-ordinator of the European Commission's teacher education initiative between 1989 and 1991.

John Clay is senior lecturer in Science Education, Brighton University. He taught in the secondary and middle school sectors in Croyden and Merton. He worked as tutor in Science Education at Thames Polytechnic before changing to his current post.

John Coldron trained as a primary teacher and taught in primary schools for twelve years. He is course leader of the Postgraduate Certificate of Education and was co-director of the TENET project at Sheffield Hallam University. He has three sons and one daughter.

Gill Crozier is a senior lecturer in Education Studies at Bath College of Higher Education. She has carried out research into the implementation of LEA policies on 'race' and education in schools and has written a number of articles on 'race' issues in education. She is a member of the Anti-Racist Teacher Education Network.

Pratap Deshpande is a policy adviser in Birmingham responsible for the needs of ethnic minority pupils in schools. He has considerable teaching experience at senior and advisory level. Pratap is a member of the Council for the Accreditation of Teacher Education, of the National Curriculum Council Working Group on Multicultural Education and of the Education Programme Advisory Group of the Polytechnics and Colleges Founding Council.

Anne Flintoff lectures in Sociology of Education and Physical Education in the Faculty of Cultural and Educational Studies at Leeds Metropolitan University. Her current PhD research reflects her commitment to raising awareness of and challenging gender inequality within teacher education and physical education.

Rosalyn George is senior lecturer in Education, West Sussex Institute of Higher Education. She has taught in both primary and middle schools in the London Boroughs of Sutton and Merton, and was an advisory teacher for equal opportunities and assessment before changing to teacher education.

Uvanney Maylor is a full-time PhD research student with the Open University, where she is also a part-time tutor counsellor. Prior to this she was a research assistant working on the National Oracy Project at Bedford College of Higher Education.

Ian Menter is director of studies for initial teacher education at the University of the West of England at Bristol. He has written a number of articles on education policy, teacher education and anti-racism. He is a member of the Anti-Racist Teacher Education Network.

Nargis Rashid is an education services adviser in Birmingham responsible for co-ordinating governor training for school governing bodies. She is a council member of the Advisory Centre for Education (ACE), and a member of the Education Committee of the Arts Council and of the Policy Committee of West Midlands Community Development Foundation. Nargis has played a major part in the national research project 'Ethnic Communities and School Governing Bodies' (1990). She has been awarded an MBE for her work.

Pat Sikes is a lecturer in the Department of Education at the University of Warwick. She has recently co-authored a book on gender and education with Lynda Measor. Her special interest is in the use of life history to study teachers' careers and she is presently using this approach to investigate how the experience of motherhood influences women teachers' perceptions, attitudes and experiences of their work.

Iram Siraj-Blatchford has taught in primary schools and nurseries. She is currently a lecturer in Education at the University of Warwick. As a black feminist she is concerned with the limitations imposed on black and female students in teacher education. Her research and publications include looking at the experiences of black students in teacher education, developing black, feminist perspectives in research and exploring cross-cultural constructions of childhood.

Gaby Weiner is professor of Education at South Bank University, having worked as a primary teacher in London and at the National Foundation for Educational Research, Schools

Council and Open University. Throughout her career as a teacher, researcher and course developer she has been concerned with putting equality issues on the educational agenda, most recently recognizing the importance of management strategies and institutional policy-making in this venture.

Series Editor's Introduction

At the time of writing, teacher education in Britain is undergoing dramatic change. Recent government policy has sought to make initial teacher education more school-based and in-service training more school-orientated. These changes have led to greater interest in teacher education generally and to increasing focus on the relationship between the school and higher education in the initial teacher training process.

Simultaneously, teacher educators and researchers have begun to accumulate understanding and expertise in the area of equal opportunities, in particular, in relation to students, curriculum, and institutional policies and practices. This has happened despite central government's apparent failure to see equality/inequality as central to recent debates about educational achievement and teacher professionalism: so much so that, having established an early lead in the development of anti-discrimination legislation, Britain is now rapidly falling behind Europe and other western countries in its equal opportunities policies and practices (see Chapter 4, and Taylor (1993)).

Going someway to redressing this imbalance, I am delighted to be able to introduce this new collection of articles which brings together the work of a wide variety of people on equal opportunities in teacher education: that of researchers, teacher trainers, senior managers and policy-makers, and local authority inspectors and advisers. The accumulated message from these contributors is that there is massive evidence that discrimination and inequality continue to permeate institutions and individuals involved in teacher education, and that change is urgent and long overdue. They further present a catalogue of strategies and practices which have been found to be central to challenging and transforming structures and practices.

It is to be hoped that as schools and higher education work towards a new framework of collaboration, they incorporate, from the start, equal opportunities philosophies and strategies in their thinking. For them, this collection is a *must* as it will give them some indication of how to pinpoint what is going wrong currently and what they can do about it. For others with a more general interest in education this volume will provide a background and update to current debates within teacher education and, in particular, on why the 'permeation' model of equal opportunities has been found to be so ineffective.

It is to be hoped, at minimum, that this volume will raise consciousness about the necessity of change within teacher education and, more optimistically, will enable the link to be established between failure to attend to such issues, and apparently more pressing concerns – of continuing national decline in world markets and in cultural achievements.

Gaby Weiner

Reference

Taylor, S. (1993) *Equal Opportunities Policies and the 1988 Education Reform Act in Britain: Equity Issues in Cultural and Political Context* (unpublished paper). School of Cultural and Policy Studies, Queensland University of Technology.

List of Abbreviations

ARTEN Anti-Racist Teacher Education Network, a voluntary network run by teacher educators in the UK which aims to promote equality.

BA(QTS) Bachelor of Arts with Qualified Teacher Status, a four-year honours degree offered by some universities leading to a teaching qualification.

BEd Bachelor of Education, a four-year honours degree resulting in Qualified Teacher Status (QTS).

CATE Council for the Accreditation of Teacher Education, a government body set up in 1984 with local committees which provides national criteria and accreditation of teacher education.

CNAA Council for National Academic Awards. A national degree-awarding body dissolved in March 1993.

CRE Commission for Racial Equality, which is concerned with the implementation of the 1976 Race Relations Act.

DES The Department for Education and Science, which in 1992 became the DFE, the Department for Education. It is the government department responsible for state education.

EOC Equal Opportunities Commission, set up to promote gender equality through the Sex Discrimination Act 1975.

ERA Education Reform Act (1988). An Act of Parliament bringing about sweeping changes in education, including the first National Curriculum for England and Wales, and changes to the powers and funding of local authorities, schools and higher education.

GEST	Grants for Educational Support and Training.
HEI	Higher Education Institutions. Usually referring to universities, polytechnics and colleges of higher education. Most HEIs became universities under new legislation in 1992.
HMI	Her Majesty's Inspectorate, responsible for inspecting educational standards from the DES/DFE.
INSET	In-Service Education Training, which is on-going professional development for practising teachers.
ITE	Initial Teacher Education, which includes the four-year BEd and PGCE.
LEA	Local Education Authority, regional area authorities with responsibility for state education.
NFER	National Foundation for Educational Research.
NUT	National Union of Teachers, one of the largest teachers' unions in Britain with members from nursery to secondary school teachers.
PGCE	Postgraduate Certificate of Education, a one-year course for graduates resulting in Qualified Teacher Status.

Setting the Scene

Reproduction or Reconstruction? Towards Equality in Teacher Education: An Introduction

IRAM SIRAJ-BLATCHFORD

The history of state education in the United Kingdom, and much of its development from its beginning to the present have been motivated, measured and justified in terms of the nation's economic and productive progress. Reforms have generally been based upon the expressed need to extend and improve provision for the masses. This emphasis upon the educational development of the nation's workforce can be seen as much in efforts to achieve comprehensive and co-educational provision as in the earlier introduction and more recent reintroduction of a differentiated system. Educational reforms have traditionally been based upon notions of underachievement, identified initially in terms of the underachievement of the economy and subsequently of that of sections of the workforce. The compensatory perspectives of the last two decades have stressed the 'deprived' conditions in which some children are reputedly socialized and emphasis here has been on the provision of extra nursery places, English language support and access to secondary education and examinations.

The emphasis has usually been on increasing the quantity or quality of knowledge and skills being transmitted, rather than on questioning the educational content and context themselves. In this respect the provisions of the 1988 Education Reform Act and

the UK National Curriculum offer nothing new. Given the
realities of a society characterized by long-established and
largely taken-for-granted inequalities of 'race', class and gender
a curriculum emphasizing mass *entitlement* is not enough on its
own. To counter inequality we need to provide an all-embracing
equalitarian *ethos* within which our children are educated. We
also need to accept an educative role with parents and the community in general. The teacher's challenge is to formulate
strategies to make knowledge and skills accessible and relevant
to children's lives and thereby a part of their everyday language
and culture.

In terms of gender and class inequality, this means confronting
sexism and privilege more directly, but this emphasis is nowhere
more apparent or widely recognized than in the education of
ethnic minority children. The Swann Report (1985), commis-
sioned in the 1970s to look at the education of children from
ethnic minority groups, argued that the underachievement of
black children was largely due to racial discrimination, particularly in employment and housing and partly in education
itself. The Swann Report made it clear that, if we were to tackle
this underachievement we must accept that we are faced with a
dual problem: first, to eradicate white racism; and second, to
provide equality of opportunity in education. These conclusions
are equally applicable to both gender inequality and the underachievement of working class children. The appendices to the
Swann Report and an ever increasing body of research evidence
(Wright 1987; 1992; Mac an Ghaill 1988; Troyna and Hatcher
1992) document the degree and nature of racism that black
children experience in the UK educational system.

The effects of teacher stereotyping, inappropriate curriculum
content and the use of racist and sexist resources in the classroom
damage children's self-images and instil in their white and male
peers false notions of superiority. Racist and sexist graffiti and
name calling, while outlawed in some schools, are still widely
prevalent outside. If black children and girls are to succeed on
equal terms with their white and male peers in our schools all of
these problems need to be tackled. So why have they not been
addressed already? The problem lies in a general lack of
understanding. Most teachers and educationalists still fail to
appreciate the effects of racism and sexism and, perhaps more
seriously, they often fail to recognize it. They certainly fail to

understand their own role in dismantling racism and sexism and the urgency of the matter. In failing to address these issues in a systematic and committed manner, teacher education has contributed to a cycle reproducing inequality in the education system in general.

While the implications of the proposed expansion of school-based initial training are included throughout the chapters, much of the discussion throughout this book is focused on initial teacher education, that is, our four-year Bachelor of Education (BEd) honours degree and one year Postgraduate Certificate of Education (PGCE) courses. However, many of the arguments adopted are more widely relevant and a specific chapter has been dedicated to in-service education. This final chapter illustrates, in a case study, a model for moving forward in a service environment where ITE, induction and professional development may be combined.

The edition of this collection has been motivated by my lived 'participant research', formal research and teaching experience. My experience and research have shown that many students (black students in particular), and tutors in teacher education are dissatisfied with the failure of teacher education to respond effectively to 'race' and gender issues.

The contributions are drawn from predominantly English contexts, and the effects of British legislation and policies provide a central focus for many of the chapters. Major themes, applicable throughout teacher education, whether it be conducted in Wales or New South Wales, Europe or the USA, provide essential strands to a common perspective. Themes such as 'student experiences', 'market-led educational reform', 'policy', 'course construction', 'admissions' and 'management' will be considered relevant to an international audience.

While aware of the continuing debates surrounding definitions of racism, anti-racism and multicultural education, black perspectives and epistemologies, and postmodern discourses of 'difference', we have chosen not to engage directly with such abstract concerns here. This book is intended as a very practical introduction to the specific issues of concern to teacher educators. To a large degree the political context in which we are involved determines our usage of such terms and progress needs to be made on a number of fronts if we are to engage with what Gramsci (1971) might have termed the ideological hegemony of racism. This issue is probably most clearly demonstrated in Deshpande and Rashid's concluding chapter where many of the 'race' equality initiatives are deliberately couched in terms considered, through experience, to be most appropriate to audiences as yet neither committed nor conversant with the subject. The perspective common to all of the contributors, despite some variation in their use of terms, is thus a strong commitment to achieving equality of opportunity in education and the recognition that this involves more than merely good will and attitude change.

The following chapters are thus dedicated to promoting equality and social justice, and for these purposes racism and sexism in teacher education are defined broadly as those beliefs, actions, procedures and practices which, intentionally or unintentionally, directly or indirectly, disadvantage female, black and other ethnic minority individuals unjustly, and as a direct consequence of their membership of those groups. The term 'black' is used mainly to refer to visible ethnic minorities of African-Caribbean and South Asian origin; it is also used as a political term which denotes the experience of racism and therefore incorporates other ethnic minority groups with similar experiences such as Turkish, Greek Cypriot and Chinese. 'Race' is held throughout in inverted commas to emphasize the problematic nature of the term; it has clearly demonstrated more historical value [sic] in oppressing certain groups than it has any scientific utility.

The contributors fully recognize that the subject of 'ethnicity' (like 'race') is highly problematic and no attempt is made here to explore the nature of this concept outside the discourse of racism. Clearly any such treatment would involve an engagement with the discourse of 'difference' and the particular needs of culturally diverse groups, this, we consider, would only provide a distraction from our main purpose of promoting just and equalitarian practice in teacher education.

Many of those individuals and bodies who have studied education for equality approaches, including HMI and the Swann Committee, have criticized the incoherent developments in teacher education. The disparate and optional nature of courses and procedures affecting staff development has led many teacher educators and students to argue that a comprehensive and holistic approach to equality needs to be provided. This book offers an exciting and comprehensive range of research-based, practical and theoretical understandings upon which policies and new practices may be formulated. The chapters emphasize the important role of teacher education, and the implications of this to students, tutors, schools and institutions of higher education.

Section 1

In the first of three sections I offer with Pat Sikes a holistic view of 'race' and gender issues and set teacher education in its wider educational context. In doing so we emphasize that although teacher education is only one part of the system, it plays a crucial part in the reproduction or reconstruction of student-teacher attitudes and understandings which are later reflected in their school and classroom practices. We illustrate the negative effects of racist and sexist attitudes and ignorance. Pam Boulton and John Coldron draw on the development of equal opportunities, defined here as largely relating to gender equality and teacher education in other European countries. They trace the background, history and current status of cross-Europe initiatives and legislation and compare the British context with other parts of Europe through projects in initial and in-service teacher education.

Section 2

This section is concerned with student experience and begins with a chapter by Maud Blair and Uvanney Maylor, based on research data collected to show the concerns of black women on a teacher education course in South East England. Blair and Maylor questioned their respondents' reasons for choosing a teaching career and study the personal and institutional factors that affected their educational experiences. The life-history approach adopted offers powerful amplification of student voices. Anne Flintoff presents original analysis of data gathered as part of a larger study on the reproduction of gender relations through the professional socialization of secondary PE teachers. Flintoff focuses on the everyday classroom interactions at one case-study institution and shows that, despite the fact that most students and staff were female, the behaviour of male students played a central part in determining the nature of classroom interaction, the ethos of the workshop sessions, and the shape and nature of course content. Each of these authors conclude by outlining policy implications and recommendations.

Gill Crozier and Ian Menter reflect on the socio-political and professional context of school-based experience for black and female students. They explore data which graphically illustrate the power relations between student, teacher and tutor and identify the main factors which inhibit 'race' and gender equality processes during school experience. They argue for political and professional alliances, as well as for the provision of guidance for students on dealing with racism and sexism in schools.

Section 3

The third section investigates the policies, strategies and changes required to promote equality in teacher education. Lynda Carr's opening chapter on admissions and outcome reveals the ways in which admissions policies reflect the equality objectives of institutions and departments. Carr cites evidence of discrimination from the Commission for Racial Equality (CRE) and Equal Opportunities Commission (EOC) and makes practical recommendations regarding the admission and selection process. Rosalyn George and John Clay argue that 'permeation' as a model for the implementation of equality practices throughout ITE courses and institutions has failed due to the pressures of the Council for the Accreditation of Teacher Education (CATE), modularization and the lack of staff commitment. George and Clay offer a model based on principles of egalitarianism and suggest that a curriculum for empowerment should be instituted, particularly for students, through the development of an 'Open Forum' which they argue would enable students to engage with and combat oppressions.

Leone Burton and Gaby Weiner draw on a research project which explored the positions and experiences of successful black and female managers and the implications for the development of social justice approaches to educational decision-making. They cite and elaborate on a number of relevant issues such as mentoring, management styles, ambience, networking and institutional profiles and make practical suggestions for action.

The final chapter by Pratap Deshpande and Nargis Rashid offers a local authority perspective. They focus on successful changes that have been achieved through in-service education and analyse the rationale that has informed these initiatives. Working with over 400 governing bodies in a major metropolitan authority, they offer their expertise in developmental work with teachers, governors, parents and the wider community. They illustrate how important it is for teacher educators to work in partnership with schools, communities and LEAs.

Each of these contributions provides valuable insights, the need for holistic perspectives, the importance of sharing experience and empowerment, the development of alliances and policy initiatives, the rejection of 'permeation' and the importance of validation and accreditation. These contributions may inform our efforts to provide equality in education together; the alternative, continued participation in the reproduction of inequality, is unthinkable.

References

Gramsci, A. (1971) *Selections from the Prison Notebooks*, ed. Q. Hoare and Nowell-Smith, Lawrence and Wishart, London.

Mac an Ghaill, M. (1988) *Young, Gifted and Black*, Open University Press, Milton Keynes.

Swann, Lord (1985) *Education for All*, HMSO, London.

Troyna, B. and Hatcher, R. (1992) *Racism in Children's Lives: A Study of Mainly-White Primary Schools*, Routledge, London, in association with the National Children's Bureau.

Wright, C. (1987) 'Black students – white teachers' in B. Troyna (ed.), *Racial Inequality in Education*, Allen and Unwin, London.

Wright, C. (1992) 'Early education, multiracial primary school classrooms' in D. Gill *et al.* (eds), *Racism and Education: Structures and Strategies*, Sage Publications, London.

CHAPTER 2

Gender and Teacher Education

PAT SIKES

I sat in your lecture on gender and education and thought, 'What a load of rubbish. Boys and girls are treated the same these days.' Then I went out on school practice and it was all 'Two strong boys to carry this table', 'Nice girls don't shout', 'Could you come and put a plug on my new printer Mr Brown?' The head and deputy and most of the people with allowances were men, though there were more women overall, and it wasn't just in my school, practically everyone else had the same experience. (Maureen, primary trainee)

You know, during this year I've listened to what's been said about gender and I've realized, to my horror, that I've tended to treat my son and daughter differently and to have different expectations of and for them. Not necessarily in big things like the jobs they might end up in, but in everyday 'ordinary' ways like putting more time into my daughter's appearance and putting my son's untidiness down to the fact he's a boy. And it's the little things that add up isn't it? (Barbara, primary trainee)

Why does all this stuff about gender matter? Surely it's always been the case that men and women are different and do different things? That's the way it is and I don't see why we should try to change it. (Sara, secondary trainee)

These three comments come from students at the end of their first year of a BA with Qualified Teacher Status (BAQTS) course. As they were unsolicited they may not be typical, nevertheless they do highlight certain issues which are central to any discussion of gender and teacher education, namely: that schools in the 1990s continue to differentiate pupils in terms of gender; that teachers and student teachers perceive boys and girls differently and have different expectations of and for them; that there are a disproportionate number of men in senior positions in schools; and that gender differences are, for some teachers and student teachers, 'common sense', taken for granted and 'natural'.

Educational inequality is a structural phenomenon. Social class, ethnic group membership, physical and cognitive facility, and gender have all been shown to influence pupils' (and teachers') experiences of school and schooling and the degree of 'success' individuals achieve (see, for example, Halsey *et al.* 1980; Spender and Sarah 1980; Walker and Barton 1983; Wright 1987). At various times legislation and official advice and recommendations have explicitly acknowledged the injustice of this and the role that schools play in maintaining and reinforcing differentiation and have given some legitimacy to the quest for equality. The 1944 and 1988 Education Acts both claimed greater equality for pupils as their prime purpose and the initial education of teachers has also received attention in this context. From its establishment in 1984 until the time of writing, the Council for the Accreditation of Teacher Education (CATE) has asserted that courses should make students aware of the 1975 Sex Discrimination Act and of the need to teach in ways that do not discriminate against children on grounds of gender or 'race'; while the DES have stated that students should 'guard against preconceptions based on the race or sex of pupils' (DES 1984, p. 11) and 'on completion of their course . . . should be . . . able to incorporate in their teaching cross-curricular dimensions (e.g. equal opportunities)' (DES 1989, p. 10).

Despite this 'official' recognition, certain right-wing critics have viewed the introduction of gender issues into teacher education as 'faddish concerns' of 'loony leftists' (Lawlor 1990). Perhaps because gender differentiation is commonly seen as 'natural' and is so much a part of the status quo, such criticisms receive far wider support than they might otherwise warrant from parents and teachers alike. The media and politicians of all parties tend to put the educational emphasis on 'improving' academic 'standards' and addressing gender and 'race' is depicted as a time-wasting diversion rather than a necessary prerequisite of academic and social achievement. At the time of writing, during the early 1990s, the Conservative government's moves to reintroduce 'traditional' teaching methods and to 'reform' teacher education have resulted in (proposed new) skills-based criteria for the approval of training courses. These criteria omit all reference to gender and 'race' equality (DES 1992).

Yet, even when required to address gender the extent to which initial teacher education (ITE) courses have done so varies greatly. And, furthermore, evidence (Skelton 1985; 1987; 1989) suggests that some courses actually reinforce gender differentiation through their hidden curriculum (see Chapter 6 by Anne Flintoff).

In 1988 the Equal Opportunities Commission (EOC) set up a formal investigation 'in order to ascertain the extent to which teacher training institutions include equal opportunities (gender) in their students' educational and professional courses' (EOC 1989, p. 5). Information was collected through a questionnaire sent to all institutions involved in ITE (to which there was a response rate of 94 per cent), follow-up discussions, observations, and responses to a general Public Notice which invited comments. The findings were that

> on paper the prospects for good equal opportunities practice in both curriculum content and the organisation and management of the institutions looked quite good. However, the reality of the situation was considerably less good, and so varied as to make generalization difficult. (EOC 1989, p. 7)

Furthermore, the investigation

> revealed, overall, an unsatisfactory situation of benign apathy towards equal opportunities. The issue was acknowledged, amongst the institutions without exception, as being a 'good thing', but in competition with 'other pressing demands' the approach of the majority of institutions was reactive and incoherent. Many institutions claimed to be carrying out programmes of work but provided no evidence or examples to substantiate their claims. (EOC 1989, p. 7)

Such findings are not, perhaps, surprising given the lack of any national detailed guidelines or criteria on what is to be covered under the heading of gender or how it is to be approached, and of any systematic and formal procedure for monitoring and assessing implementation. Such guidelines were recommended by the Commission. At the institutional level, an equal opportunities policy which is monitored and assessed seemed more likely to be accompanied by action on equal opportunities, but not all institutions have such a policy.

Teacher training courses, whether they be one-year PGCEs or four-year BEd/BAQTSs, have to cover a great deal of content. If equal opportunities are not seen as a priority they may get squeezed out. In some institutions gender issues are tacked on to existing courses. One or two lectures deal with equal opportunities as a separate matter from the 'mainstream' course content. It may be that this kind of token approach does more harm than good in that it can result in marginalization in so far as students may see 'gender' as a separate issue which is not of central concern in their own practice. Another approach is to offer equal opportunities as an optional or extra course. This means that it is not presented as being of significance for all teachers. This impression is also given if only those students preparing to teach a particular age group receive equal opportunities input. The EOC investigation found that gender issues were more frequently raised on secondary courses than on primary ones. This could be partly due to the greater number of subject areas CATE requires primary students to cover (i.e. 'other pressing demands'), and also to the mistaken idea that equal opportunities are not an issue in primary education (cf. Troyna and Hatcher 1992).

In response to time constraints some institutions have adopted a permeation model. In other words, they claim to address equal opportunities right across and through their curriculum. Since gender issues do permeate all aspects and areas of school life, the permeation model is, theoretically, very appropriate. If carefully monitored and assessed, permeation could be highly successful (Hanson 1987). However, in some cases the EOC investigators

> were unconvinced that those concerned knew what they were permeating, to whom, or why. A permeation model alone cannot be satisfactory unless equal opportunities has a very high profile of its own in the training programme, built on skills, knowledge, a positive attitude and an active approach to learning. (EOC 1989, p. 9)

The lack of systematic assessment of gender input on ITE courses is, of course, significant. While the EOC found that 'in general, institutions recognized the need for gender awareness' there was little evidence that 'raising awareness was influencing the way that students were preparing to teach' (EOC 1989, p. 8). In any case it would be naive to take the view that awareness and knowledge prompts action. Gender differentiation, in all its forms, is so deep-rooted and ingrained in most people's consciousness and ways of behaving that there has to be a real commitment to self-conscious reflection in order to change habits which have become taken for granted. Even when this exists 'mistakes' can still be made, as anyone who has watched a video recording of him/herself teaching will confirm. Awareness and knowledge are not enough: teachers need to have access to resources and to be equipped with strategies which actively promote equal opportunities. These strategies could be included in any competence-based course requirements but for this to happen structural sexism has to be acknowledged and gender differentiation needs to be recognized as a real 'problem' which constrains and limits the opportunities and achievements of all boys and girls, men and women. This acknowledgement and recognition is not yet apparent.

Without any formal criteria to meet, what institutions provide with regard to equal opportunities can very much depend upon the commitment of individuals. This is especially true when no equal opportunities policy exists. This means that there is often a lack of co-ordination and that equal opportunities courses can collapse when committed individuals leave. It also means that if staff are hostile towards gender issues, as the EOC investigation found was sometimes the case, their coverage is obviously affected.

As in schools, senior staff in institutions of higher education tend to be male, white and middle-class. Heward (1991) cites the figures of senior staff in the education faculty of one university as exemplifying male domination in teacher education: although 80 per cent of students in the faculty were women, 65 per cent of lecturers and 93 per cent of senior lecturers, readers and professors were men. She suggests that this has little to do with the respective abilities of men and women but is more a consequence of the shift from single-sex to mixed teacher education, and the way in which 'managerial authority, seen as overwhelmingly masculine, has been legitimated in promotion to senior positions'. This male domination is significant not only in terms of women's promotion prospects but also with regard to the role models available to staff and students.

Research suggests that senior male managers tend to prefer 'authoritarian' forms of management (Al-Khalifa 1989). These forms involve 'aggressive, competitive behaviours, emphasis on control rather than negotiation and collaboration, and the pursuit of competition rather than shared problem solving' (Al-Khalifa 1989, p. 89). These behaviours are closely linked to masculine attitudes and values and, within an institution, their practice results in a masculine ethos. Concern about the implications and effects of such an ethos have led some schools to experiment with more collaborative and personal management styles: styles which are more in tune with what are regarded as feminine characteristics. Indeed, research in American schools has revealed that 'achievement in reading and maths is higher . . . there is less violence and . . . staff and student morale is higher' (Shakeshaft 1986, p. 153) when women occupy the senior management positions.

While institutions providing teacher education are not American high schools they generally are male-dominated and male-orientated, and students (and staff) are consciously and unconsciously influenced by this and their experiences are shaped by it. As Caroline Benn writes:

> Historically, there have always been two distinct teaching functions: the first an extension of mothering, and reserved for women; the second an extension of power and authority, reserved for men, who have guarded it well. This division – while no longer explicit – is still important throughout the education system. (Benn 1989, p. xix)

In many institutions this division can be clearly seen: staff and students on courses preparing primary school teachers (traditionally seen as a maternal-type job) tend to be female, while those on secondary courses tend to be male. In addition, students and staff tend to work on and take subject courses which are regarded as traditional for their sex. This does have implications for the situation in schools because it means that the traditional associations are maintained and pupils continue to be presented with traditional role models.

The EOC survey sought to discover whether any institutions employed specific measures to encourage male and female students to enter non-traditional areas. This question was based on the hypothesis that 'if an institution were aware of issues relating to gender equality then they might use the sections of the SDA [Sex Discrimination Act] which encourage positive action or take other special measures' (EOC 1989, p. 28). The findings were that 19 per cent took action to encourage women into Craft, Design and Technology, 13 per cent tried to encourage men to train to become infant teachers, and another 19 per cent claimed to take 'general' action by such measures as targeting publicity materials, modified interview procedures, open days and distance learning materials. However, there was no indication of how successful these actions were, perhaps because they were not systematically monitored.

With regard to encouraging mature students, 76 per cent of institutions took action in terms of special entry qualifications, access courses and encouragement for mature women. It is perhaps significant to note that institutions with an equal opportunities policy were more likely to take steps to encourage mature entrants than those without. No information was given about positive action to recruit women from black and ethnic minority groups so this may be an area which has yet to be addressed.

The EOC survey did not collect evidence about female student teachers' experiences as women in institutions of higher education. There is, however, no reason to suppose that these are not the same as in any other work place or sector of society: 'Sexual harassment has been considered normal behaviour in the relationship between men and women at work throughout history' (Sedley and Benn 1984, p. 5). Indeed, research indicates that female teachers and pupils in schools are sexually harassed by male teachers and pupils (Woods 1979; Ball 1987; Burgess 1989; Cunnison 1989; De Lyon 1989, Herbert 1989) and that women students in universities are sexually harassed by male lecturers (Dzeich and Weiner 1984). Sexual harassment may range from sexual joking and innuendo through to propositioning and actual physical assault. Dzeich and Weiner found that some male lecturers offered higher marks for sexual favours and if these were not granted gave low marks or even failed students.

Sexual harassment is about power, and women, generally, have less power, both in terms of their physical strength and with regard to their authority within a school or institution of higher education. Consequently, when they experience harassment they may be reluctant to complain for fear of jeopardizing their future. In addition, they may doubt that their complaint will be taken seriously because it is not unusual for behaviour of this kind to be seen as 'natural' and 'normal' for men and something which women should learn to put up with. In one institution a male student teacher who indecently exposed himself to a female lecturer was defended by his male course tutor on the grounds that his behaviour was just the 'natural' and 'normal' result of Saturday night overindulgence. Of course, the existence of an equal opportunities policy should act as a safeguard but, as we have seen, not all institutions possess one and, if they do, do not necessarily put it in to operation. There is also the difficulty of proving intent, which puts many women off making complaints in the first place.

Women generally have responsibility for childcare, yet the EOC found no mention of crèche/nursery facilities or adaptations to the timetable to make things easier for students or staff with family commitments. While staff are entitled to at least statutory provision for maternity leave, the position is less clear for students. Only a very small proportion of students actually become pregnant during their course, nevertheless this does not excuse the total neglect of the possibility by institutions who have no provision for granting students maternity leave. Of two cases in different institutions known to the author, one student was given 'sick leave', and the other was expected to continue the course and 'work round the birth' or repeat the entire year.

So what sort of attitudes with regard to gender do intending teachers have? We can only assume that they are the same as other members of the population. Thus, as a result of their own socialization and their experiences in and outside school it is perhaps not surprising that research shows that many student teachers hold 'deeply entrenched and pernicious . . . sexually differentiated educational expectations for boys and girls' (Spender and Sarah 1982, p. 138; see also Skelton and Hanson 1989). Indeed Delamont (1991) goes as far as to suggest that male and female students and practising teachers are likely to hold traditional, conservative views about sex roles as a result of their family backgrounds.

An investigation involving 155 first-year students on a BAQTS course found that over 25 per cent of them expected boys, but not girls, to be reckless, untidy, cheeky, brave, noisy and naughty; and expected girls, but not boys, to be tidy, clean, quiet, sensible, obedient, passive and well behaved (Sikes 1991). Such findings are disturbing if, as seems likely,

> where teachers hold such expectations about the interests, abilities, conduct and personalities of their male and female pupils . . . they may, by the encouragement they give and the stimuli they provide, heighten any such differences as may exist and create special problems for the boy or girl who does not conform to type. (Stanworth 1981, p. 21)

The responsibility that teacher educators have to provide a challenge to conventional, taken-for-granted understandings and assumptions concerning gender, is clearly great. Unfortunately much of the evidence suggests that ITE has a relatively weak influence on teachers' ideas and practices (cf. Dale 1977; Denscombe 1985; Acker 1987; Lee 1987; Quicke, 1988).

Once student teachers are in school, whether on school practice or in a job, the paramount need is to survive. Even those who hold equalitarian views and who are committed to equal opportunities may find that once they get into schools and classrooms the practical exigencies of the situation may seem to be best tackled by strategies which contradict and conflict with their personal beliefs (Hanson and Hetherington 1976; Clarricoates 1980a; 1980b; Whyte 1983; Sikes *et al*. 1985; Acker 1988; Menter 1989). In addition to actually teaching and being with pupils, students and new teachers have to establish relationships with colleagues: they have to be socialized into the occupational and institutional culture and learn how to be a 'proper' teacher. By observation and experience they learn what is considered appropriate within their particular school. If they are to pass their school-based experience (Menter 1989) or have a smooth-running career (Hanson and Hetherington 1976, pp. 6–7), it is as well to fit in and to internalize or at least strategically comply (see Lacey 1977, pp. 72–3) with the informal yet important rules. As Lacey noted, when new teachers had to pass a probationary year, those who questioned, rejected, or attempted to change what was regarded as appropriate professional behaviour, could experience 'serious problems in qualifying' (Lacey 1977, p. 96).

Attitudes and practices relating to gender are an aspect of professional behaviour and teachers can have very strong feelings about what is appropriate. Some schools are, of course, deeply committed to equal opportunities and have policies and take action to monitor and evaluate them. Many others do not. There is a considerable and growing body of evidence which indicates that many teachers unconsciously and consciously hold sexist attitudes which are translated into their practices (cf. Lafrance 1991). At an anecdotal level students regularly return from school practice and tell of girl pupils being expected to do all the tidying up, boy pupils doing all the furniture moving, and teachers who tell them that concern with equal opportunities is left-wing theory and/or a waste of time because all differences between the sexes are 'natural'. Teacher educators supervising school practices have similar experiences and often, given the need to maintain good relationships with the schools that take their students, also fail to speak out, or to stop students going to that school. Given this context it is perhaps not surprising that Menter's research should have led him to conclude that:

> Teaching practice is characterized by 'stasis', a strong tendency for those most closely involved to avoid conflict or confrontation. Even mild criticism of existing classroom practices is avoided. To the extent that approaches to the appraisal of practising teachers are based on similar 'supervisory' models, the implication is that the effect will not be the 'development' or 'improvement' of practice so much as the reinforcement of existing practices whether good or bad. (Menter 1989, p. 459)

This 'stasis' and 'reinforcement of existing practices' becomes even more significant and disturbing if and when, as is planned, schools take greater responsibility for teacher education. It will be a brave student or articled teacher who dares to question, let alone speak out against, sexist practices. And it may well be that equal opportunities will receive even less attention in school-based ITE than the EOC survey found was the case in college-based courses. There are various reasons why this happens but until schemes are in operation and have been evaluated these can only remain at the level of conjecture. However, it is almost certainly the case that the day-to-day demands of school life will mean that gender issues will have to compete with 'other pressing demands', as was found to be the case in the teacher education institutions.

In school-based ITE so much depends upon the attitudes and knowledge of the teachers involved – and upon the training that those designated as 'mentors' receive. As we have already seen, teachers can and do hold sexist views and can and do consciously and unconsciously differentiate pupils on the basis of their sex in a detrimental fashion. Even those teachers who are concerned to be equalitarian may not know what they can do. The introduction of systems of appraisal which encourage and support critical reflection and which are able to provide teachers with the training and resources they need, could help (cf. Smyth 1991). However, as Menter (1989) suggests, some appraisal schemes are likely to lead to stasis. In addition, to date, provision for in-service training on gender within schools has been patchy, and is likely to become even more so under Local Management of Schools (LMS) and in grant-maintained schools. This is because headteachers will have greater control over how money is spent and they may well give priority to other areas and issues. Some LEAs have devoted more time and resources to input on gender than have others – and take-up of opportunities, where offered, has frequently been optional. There is some evidence to suggest that in-service work on gender has relatively low status and is most likely to be taken up by women and people committed to equal opportunities (Sikes 1987). This obviously restricts its impact. In addition, relatively little has been done to combat sexism in schools: it has been notoriously difficult to implement the Sex Discrimination Act and female teachers and pupils have often got nowhere with claims of unfair treatment or sexual harassment even if they have dared or bothered to speak out about it.

The students who come into teaching have already experienced the sexism of the education system at first hand, although they may personally have no complaints or may not recognize the inequities. Surely it is the job of those concerned with ITE to encourage the questioning of gender-related, taken-for-granted assumptions which have been shown to limit and constrain the potential of pupils and teachers? It is also imperative that students be provided with strategies and resources which can actually be used in classroom and school situations. Above all, ITE institutions and schools receiving students need to develop equal opportunities policies and assiduously monitor and evaluate them.

References

Acker, S. (1987) 'Primary school teaching as an occupation' in S. Delamont (ed.), *The Primary School Teacher*, Falmer, Lewes.

Acker, S. (1988) 'Teachers, gender and resistance', *British Journal of Sociology of Education*, vol. 9, no. 3, pp. 307–22.

Al-Khalifa, E. (1989) 'Management by halves: women teachers and school management' in H. De Lyon and F. Widdowson Migniuolo (eds), *Women Teachers: Issues and Experiences*, Open University Press, Milton Keynes.

Ball, S. (1987) *The Micro-politics of the School*, Methuen, London.

Benn, C. (1989) 'Preface' in H. De Lyon and F. Widdowson Migniuolo (eds), *Women Teachers: Issues and Experiences*, Open University Press, Milton Keynes.

Burgess, R. (1989) ' "Something you learn to live with"? Gender and inequality in the secondary school', *Gender and Education*, vol. 1, no. 2.

Clarricoates, K. (1980a) 'All in a day's work' in D. Spender and E. Sarah (eds), *Learning To Lose*, Women's Press, London.

Clarricoates, K. (1980b) 'The importance of being Earnest . . . Emma . . . Tom . . . Jane: The perception and categorization of gender conformity and gender in primary schools' in R. Deem (ed.), *Schooling For Women's Work*, Routledge and Kegan Paul, London.

Cunnison, S. (1989) 'Gender joking in the staffroom' in S. Acker (ed.), *Teachers, Gender and Careers*, Falmer, Lewes.

Dale, R. (1977) *The Structural Context of Teaching*, Course E202, Unit 5, Block 1, Open University Educational Enterprises, Milton Keynes.

Delamont, S. (1991) *Sex Roles and the School*, Routledge, London.

De Lyon, H. (1989) 'Sexual harassment' in H. De Lyon and F. Widdowson Migniuolo (eds), *Women Teachers: Issues and Experiences*, Open University Press, Milton Keynes.

Denscombe, M. (1985) *Classroom Control: A Sociological Perspective*, Allen and Unwin, London.

DES (1984) *ITT: Approval of Courses*, Circular No. 3/84, 13 April.

DES (1989) 'Future arrangements for the accreditation of courses of initial teacher education: a consultative document', Circular 24/82, HMSO, London.

DES (1992) *Reform of Initial Teacher Education: A Consultation Document*, 28 January.

Dzeich, B. and Weiner, L. (1984) *The Lecherous Professor: Sexual Harassment On Campus*, Beacon Press, Boston.

EOC (1989) *Formal Investigation Report on Initial Teacher Training in England and Wales*, EOC, Manchester.

Halsey, A.H., Heath, A.F. and Ridge, J.M. (1980) *Origins and Destinations*, Clarendon Press, London.

Hanson, D. and Hetherington, M. (1976) *From College to Classroom: The Probationary Year*, Routledge and Kegan Paul, London.

Hanson, J. (1987) 'Equality issues, permeation and a PGCE programme', unpublished MEd dissertation, University of Sheffield.

Herbert, C. (1989) *Talking Silence: The Sexual Harassment of Schoolgirls*, Falmer, London.

Heward, C. (1991) *Men and Women and the Rise of Professional Society: The Intriguing History of Teacher Educators*.

Heward, C. (1993) 'Men and women and the rise of professional society: the intriguing history of women educators', *History of Education*, vol. 22, no. 1, Spring.

Lacey, C. (1977) *The Socialization of Teachers*, Methuen, London.

Lafrance, M. (1991) 'School for scandal: different educational experiences for females and males', *Gender and Education*, vol. 3, no. 1, pp. 3–13.

Lawlor, S. (1990) *Teachers Mistaught: Training in Theories or Education in Subjects?* Centre for Policy Studies, London.

Lee, J. (1987) 'Pride and prejudice and an inner-city infants school' in M. Lawn and G. Grace (eds), *Teachers: The Culture and Politics of Work*, Falmer, Lewes.

Menter, I. (1989) 'Teaching practice stasis: racism, sexism and school experience in initial teacher education', *British Journal of Sociology of Education*, vol. 10, no. 4, pp. 459–73.

Quicke, J. (1988) 'Using structured life histories to teach the sociology and social psychology of education: an evaluation' in P. Woods and A. Pollard (eds), *Sociology and Teaching: A New Challenge for the Sociology of Education*, Croom Helm, London.

Sedley, A. and Benn, M. (1984) *Sexual Harassment at Work*, National Council for Civil Liberties, Rights For Women Unit, London.

Shakeshaft, C. (1986) 'A gender at risk', *Phi Delta Kappa*, March.

Sikes, P.J. (1987) 'Take up of INSET in – LEA', unpublished paper for – LEA.

Sikes, P.J. (1991) ' "Nature took its course"?: student teachers and gender awareness', *Gender and Education*.

Sikes, P.J., Measor, L. and Woods, P. (1985) *Teacher Careers: Crises and Continuities*, Falmer, Lewes.

Skelton, C. (1985) 'Gender issues in a PGCE teacher training programme', unpublished MA thesis, University of York.

Skelton, C. (1987) 'A study of gender discrimination in a primary programme of teacher training', *Journal of Education for Teaching*, vol. 13, no. 2, pp. 163–75.

Skelton, C. (1989) 'And so the wheel turns . . . gender and initial teacher education' in C. Skelton (ed.), *Whatever Happens to Little Women?*, Open University Press, Milton Keynes.

Skelton, C. and Hanson, J. (1989) 'Schooling the teachers: gender and initial teacher education' in S. Acker (ed.), *Teachers, Gender and Careers*, Falmer, Lewes.

Smyth, J. (1991) *Teachers as Collaborative Learners*, Open University Press, Milton Keynes.

Spender, D, and Sarah, E. (eds) (1980) *Learning To Lose: Sexism and Education*, The Women's Press, London.

Spender, D. and Sarah, E. (1982) 'An investigation of the implications of courses on sex discrimination in teacher education' in S. Acker and D. Warren Piper (eds), *Is Higher Education Unfair to Women?* SRHE and NFER Nelson, Guildford.

Stanworth, M. (1981) *Gender and Schooling: A Study of Sexual Divisions in the Classroom*, Hutchinson, London.

Troyna, B. and Hatcher, R. (1992) *Racism In Children's Lives: A Study of Mainly-White Primary Schools*, Routledge, London.

Walker, S. and Barton, L. (eds) (1983) *Gender, Class and Education*, Falmer, Lewes.

Whyte, J. (1983) 'Sex differences and sex typing', *Journal of Education for Teaching*, vol. 9, no. 3, pp. 235–48.

Woods, P. (1979) *The Divided School*, Routledge and Kegan Paul, London.

Wright, C. (1987) 'Black students, white teachers' in B. Troyna (ed.), *Racial Inequality In Education*, Tavistock, London.

CHAPTER 3

Racial Equality and Effective Teacher Education

IRAM SIRAJ-BLATCHFORD

While multicultural approaches have gained ground in recent years, anti-racism in education is still widely perceived as a product of the 'loony left' (Troyna 1987), and as the inquiry into the murder of 14-year-old Ahmed Iqbal in his school playground, a school that expressed some pride in its multicultural policies, reported:

> It has become ever more evident to us that anti-racism in symbolic gestures is meaningless and can clearly reinforce racism. If the school does not involve the total community, teachers, ancillary staff, students and parents, both black and white, in the efforts to tackle racism in school the whole exercise will end in failure. (MacDonald *et al.* 1989, p. 347)

This conclusion is as true for ITE institutions as it is for schools. MacDonald *et al.* (1989) argue that policies need to embrace at a practical and theoretical level the sub-cultural experiences of the student population. Token 'consultation' with community leaders and the implementation of multi-cultural education are inadequate in themselves.

If we want to promote equality through education, whether we are considering inequality in schools, in departments of higher education or in society in general, ITE must respond by addressing the future needs of student teachers. Unfortunately, as Michael Day suggests in a 1989 Commission for Racial Equality occasional paper (CRE 1989a):

> What is apparent is that compared with schools, universities and

polytechnics have been relatively untouched by the debate on racial equality in education and have not, on the whole, seen the need to develop specific policies in this area. It may be that these institutions have seen themselves as incapable of discrimination or unequal treatment, and thus absolved from discussions of inequality in access to educational opportunity. (p. 5)

ITE institutions are still failing to include in their courses adequate treatment of 'race', gender and class issues. ITE has also failed so far to recognize the central issues of inequality, let alone to deal with them effectively. In a 1988 Occasional Paper, the Anti-Racist Teacher Education Network (ARTEN) discussed the viability of 'permeation' as a model for change in ITE institutions, as the document states:

> Consensus in our society is achieved through the suppression of struggles based on race, class and gender. The institutional reality for those concerned about promoting genuine antiracist perspectives in schools and colleges is that permeation as a model for change cannot work whilst it is being "implemented" by people who have not raised their own consciousness and understanding of issues of 'race' and racism. (ARTEN 1988, p. 4)

In 1989 a Commission for Racial Equality survey of the equal opportunities policies in 68 universities and polytechnics found many institutions to have a 'tone of moral superiority or complacency plus ignorance of the issues' (CRE 1989b). If ITE institutions lack the necessary understanding, whom can we turn to? Who in the education system has such an understanding?

The Swann Report (1985) has stressed the urgent need for black teachers in Britain's mainstream schools, and the report commented on the problems associated with recruitment. Both racism in schools and the restricted career opportunities open to black teachers were cited. As the Report argued, white as well as black children need to be offered positive black role models. They need to be in contact with black people that have gained professional status and who command respect. Unfortunately, a CRE (1988a) survey revealed that where black teachers were employed they were generally on lower than average salaries, they tended to be in shortage subjects and they were on average older than their white colleagues.

Black teachers are needed in education. In common with the role suggested for black teachers in schools by Swann, the HMI report on *Responses to Ethnic Diversity in Teacher Training* (DES 1989b) suggests that black students act as a catalyst for change in ITE, improving awareness of anti-racism issues and offering black perspectives during seminars. The effects upon, and the feeling of, the black students given these involuntary responsibilities has never been documented. It is clear that for many they are perceived as racist (Mac an Ghaill 1988; Siraj-Blatchford 1991); a more conscious and proactive response is thus required of teacher educators in order to positively promote racial equality.

Despite these harsh realities, there is no doubt that the education system needs black teachers' multilingual expertise, their understanding of racism and also their ability to communicate this understanding to white colleagues. Both children and their teachers need black teachers as positive academic role models. Black teachers have an integral part to play in our educational community, so why do we have so few?

The shortage of black and ethnic minority teachers in Britain has been widely recognized. The Department of Education and Science has a clear policy to increase the supply of ethnic minority teachers through specially focused courses of training. However, bi- and multilingual teachers qualified abroad have often not been awarded 'Qualified Teacher Status'. Institutions have begun to look at the possibility of shortened two-year Bachelor of Education (BEd) courses or specialist postgraduate courses. A few institutions are already offering these.

A survey of black teachers in eight local education authorities (LEAs) (CRE 1988a) has estimated that black teachers make up only 2 per cent of the teaching force, compared with a 4.4 per cent black representation in the population as a whole. Indeed, it is clear that these figures understate the problem as the average age of the black population is lower, and the young tend to be better qualified and are more likely to be in non-manual employment.

Since the formation of the Committee for the Accreditation of Teacher Education (CATE), BEd courses in particular have been forced to change (DES 1989a). The emphasis on students having to study their chosen main subject to a high academic and specialist level has resulted in students spending 50 per cent of their course time on their specialism. In many cases this has more than doubled the time previously spent on specialist study. This has meant a cut in other course areas. The curriculum-studies aspect of courses has been cut marginally, but the most drastic cut in hours has been made to those courses which have traditionally dealt with the social factors which influence children's learning, the two main areas being education and teaching/professional studies (hours have been more than halved in many cases) and some school-based work. In most institutions the one-year Postgraduate Certificate in Education (PGCE) course follows a similar course content to the BEd yet even less time is available to cover these issues.

The problem with the PGCE route has been the small numbers of black students applying. Many mature adults cannot afford to do a course; those who obtained their first degree abroad have often been unable to get a grant for a PGCE, and that facility has now been completely removed. Those few access courses that have been introduced have proved to be a great success. Black students remain underrepresented in ITE and are particularly underrepresented in universities. According to research conducted by the University Central Council on Admissions (UCCA) published in July 1991 and reported in the *Times Higher Education Supplement* (21 June 1991), UK universities are currently rejecting half of *all* their black applicants. In defending the universities against any claim of racial bias, UCCA suggests: 'It will be seen that applicants from all minority ethnic groups have lower average scores than white applicants.' According to UCCA black applicants with five points or less would be more successful if they applied for places on BEd courses which accept lower scores. UCCA suggests that the high proportion of applications to high-demand courses such as Law and Medicine reduce black applicants' chances of success, that applicants who have gained their qualifications after 'several attempts' are discriminated against and that black applicants often reduce their chances of a place by applying to their local university.

As a result of a projected population slump in the mid-1990s, Britain is now beginning to run out of potential students in the 18–20 age range. One solution that has been put forward by government is the wholesale adoption of licensed and articled teachers, employed by the LEAs and provided with training during service. While such an arrangement might attract mature candidates into teaching, the scheme may simply produce a body of second-class teachers. LEAs may have the option to pay them as qualified or unqualified teachers. Indeed, under the provisions of the Education Reform Act 1988, in schools of more than 200 pupils it is now the governors who make the appointments and differentiation is being encouraged. In the long term we need to do more to recruit potential students directly from schools. Some institutions, such as Roehampton in London, are doing this effectively already. Individual institutions need direct links with schools that have ethnic minority children in the same way as Oxford and Cambridge have always had direct links with the schools from which their students are drawn.

Despite those efforts that have been made, black students have been reluctant to enter the teaching profession. The under-representation of black teachers in the UK cannot be accounted for by social class differences alone. In fact, research suggests that black parents place an even greater value on education than white parents. Working-class South Asians, for example, appear to aspire to higher education to the same extent as their middle-class peers (Gupta 1977; Kitwood and Borrell 1980; Brennan and McGeevor 1990).

Unfortunately, the national concern over the supply of ethnic minority teachers has only recently prompted the DES (now the DFE) to apply ethnic monitoring strategies. A clear picture of student applications and appointments will thus only begin to emerge in the mid-1990s. However, the CRE informed the Education, Science and Arts committee of the House of Commons (CRE 1989a) that there is unlikely to be any increase in the supply of black teachers in the 1990s. The CRE suggested that the racism and racial discrimination experienced by black students at all levels within and outside the education system was to blame.

A survey by Singh (1988) on South Asian and white sixth-formers' perceptions of the teaching profession found that well-qualified South Asian pupils cited racism among pupils and staff as a major deterrent to entering teacher education. Morrison and McIntyre (1976) cite research where suitably qualified pupils comment on the monotony of teachers' work, their low pay, discipline problems and poor promotion prospects as reasons for not entering the profession. Unsurprisingly, teachers and student-teachers have generally been found to be those who gained positive educational experiences themselves (Morrison and McIntyre 1976). In her study of eight black (African-Caribbean) women in higher education, Tomlinson (1983) found that all but one of these students felt that they had had special encouragement from their teachers.

Table 3.1 Identified sources of racism

Category specified	Racism identified by black students	
	%	No.
During teaching practice	69	48
From fellow students	64	45
In courses	44	31
From lecturers	40	28
In the administration	30	21
In resources	24	16
Accommodation	10	7
From other staff	9	6

A survey of black ITE student perceptions of racism in United Kingdom institutions (Siraj-Blatchford 1991) has shown that, far from making black students welcome, ITE institutions have contributed to the alienation of potential recruits. Of the seventy responses to this survey, only five questionnaires were returned without supplying evidence of students' perceptions of racism. Table 3.1 gives an indication of the wide range of concerns that ITE institutions need to address.

According to ARTEN (1988) ITE has typically been reactive to local school populations. Where black and ethnic minority pupils were seen to make up large proportions of some teaching practice schools a need to incorporate multi-cultural approaches had been recognized (Tomlinson 1986). This has usually been limited to the recognition of a need to know and understand ethnic minority cultures. As Swann (1985) observed, teacher education has confused two distinct forms of provision: on the one hand, provision designed to prepare students to teach in a 'multi-racial' school and, on the other hand, preparation for students to teach in a 'multi-racial' *society*. UK institutions tend to offer multi-cultural education options for those students who plan to teach in multi-ethnic schools. Multi-cultural courses are still seen by students and lecturers as an exploration of the problems faced by black people (Giles and Cherrington 1981), while the wider context of societal racism and the role of white people is largely ignored. There is a need for courses in a multi-cultural society to be concerned with providing understandings of 'race', equality and power structures as well as cultural factors (Milner 1983; Troyna 1987).

The questions that are used to select and reject students at interview are particularly significant and revealing. While there has been little research carried out in ITE, the CRE (1986b) inquiry of St George's medical school in London has shown how the chances of black candidates' reaching the interview stage have been hampered in at least one institution by a discriminatory points system. Some medical institutions have even operated quota systems! (see Collier and Burke 1986). Black students are often asked about their religion, family life, forms of dress and marital prospects when they are interviewed for ITE (Siraj-Blatchford 1991).

The CRE publication *Learning in Terror* (1987) has shown some of the effects that racial harassment has on the everyday life of black children. Racism is always damaging in an educational context. It undermines self-esteem (Milner 1983) and often leads to resistance and consequent underachievement (Wright 1987). The effects of direct and indirect racism from teachers and lecturers are especially menacing, as material injury is likely to be added to the insult. Assessments are likely to be affected.

Research carried out by Cohen (1989) on perceptions relating to ethnic minorities in Britain held by 392 first-year student teachers found that while the majority supported cultural pluralism, they generally showed considerable ignorance about ethnic minority groups. Virtually no knowledge of the history of recent settlement in Britain, or of the customs, languages and religions of ethnic minorities was evident. A small number of students were also identified who were defined as racially prejudiced. Cohen discussed his findings with students:

> It was generally acknowledged (and regretted) that there are student teachers who are racially prejudiced. Many group members expressed genuine concern lest they themselves exhibit prejudice of which they are unaware . . . there was common concern that teachers need to be selected in respect of certain characteristics, not least, that they should be free from prejudice.

Students also felt that they required more multi-cultural courses, in particular courses that were less didactic, where more discussion was allowed.

The cumulative effect of racist peer and tutor behaviour can only be estimated, but it may well contribute to the number of students who fail to survive this degradation: those who leave during or immediately after ITE.

There is some evidence to suggest that black British students perceived overseas black students as experiencing even more racism. This may be an important area for further research, given the increasing dependence of some UK institutions on overseas funding. Despite the fact that discrimination is outlawed by the Race Relations Act (1976), racism in housing in the UK is still prevalent and convictions are notoriously difficult to obtain. There is some evidence that such discriminatory practices still involve accommodation *within* ITE institutions (Siraj-Blatchford 1991) and black students need support from their student services to help with these eventualities.

School practice provides the worst experiences of racial discrimination for most black students. Institutions have failed to help black students prepare for this in any way. As Menter (1989) has pointed out, 'stasis' is a dominant feature of all teaching practice experiences. While school experience is widely recognized as a particularly influential part of the professional socialization of student teachers, current practice does not encourage open discussion and collaboration between teacher, student and tutor. At the same time, black students are acutely aware of any racism and racial stereotyping faced by black pupils (Siraj-Blatchford 1991).

In 1986–87 Her Majesty's Inspectorate of Schools (DES 1989b) inspected 16 ITE institutions to see what it is that informed and represented good practice. They later reported that they had found good practice where:

1 There was a policy document which heightened awareness especially when the staff had been involved in its formulation.
2 Policies were monitored.
3 Accommodation was provided for focusing resources at the early stages of implementation.
4 Tutors had first-hand experience of teaching in multi-ethnic schools.
5 There was a co-ordinating post, a named person like an adviser in an LEA with an appropriate level of seniority.
6 Speakers were brought in from the communities.

7 There were students from the ethnic minorities in the institution to raise issues.
8 Adequate time was given to allow a proper consideration of multi-ethnic issues within the core of courses.
9 Students were given direct experience of multi-ethnic schools.
10 Multi-ethnic issues were *not* related to issues of 'special needs'.

The ethos of all schools and colleges is of utmost importance to the black students that currently attend them, and to those who might be encouraged to enter them. Unfortunately, we still do not have enough research evidence to show how many black students fail to complete their courses, are failed, drop out of teaching practice or never go into teaching after qualifying. There is also an urgent need for more black staff in ITE. This will only come about if we effect the following changes: we need to enable students to examine attitudes and teaching strategies and methods in all courses; if this is to be achieved, then all courses need to be staffed accordingly. White racists should not be recruited into the profession, students and staff in teacher education institutions should be required to answer questions on equality of opportunity when interviewed and all staff should receive ongoing anti-racism training. Students must be taught the importance of sharing the child's community, as too many inner-city teachers come in from outside and never really perceive the needs of the community group, they impose their own values and perspectives in education. Teachers need to break down the barriers of professionalism to meet the needs of their children and parents. We need to teach student teachers diagnostic approaches rather than prescriptive ones. Teachers in suburban and predominantly white schools need to recognize the importance of anti-racist approaches to their own work.

White students need to understand the 'black experience', and this should not be interpreted or taught as a cultural or ethnic experience; they need to understand the realities of the day-to-day lives of black people living within the confines of white social practices, norms and structures. Teacher education institutions and schools need to develop clear racial harassment policies.

The level of racism in schools, from some teachers, from pupils and from lecturers within ITE, and documented in the following chapters, suggests that staff development and the appraisal of school placements and teacher mentors is not a luxury; it must now be seen as a necessary and integral part of departmental policy.

There is obviously a need for ITE to assimilate and incorporate black perspectives. In the light of present attitudes, behaviours and power structures we need to develop an historical understanding of black experience and its relation to the white experience. The black perspective needs to be part and parcel of course structures. Swann (1985) suggested that very few institutions offered a core course on anti-racism, let alone any cross-curricular permeation. This would involve monitoring all course content, as well as the more subtle aspects of institutional ethos such as texts, displays and teaching styles.

Policy statements are necessary but require clear procedures for identifying and dealing with racial discrimination. Policies are useless without real understanding; open discussion should be continuous among staff, students and the local community. The monitoring of such policies should be co-ordinated by a senior member of staff. Further research may be useful in identifying, analysing and sharing good practice. Procedures need to be developed and monitored which encompass students, the selection procedures of both staff and students, accommodation, courses and lectures. White students need to be made aware of these policies and the disciplinary implications. Ongoing review of progress is essential.

References

ARTEN (1988) 'A survey of antiracist practice in teacher education institutions in the South West and Wales' in ARTEN (eds), *Anti-racist Teacher Education, Permeation: the Road to Nowhere*, Occasional Paper 4, Jordanhill College of Education, Glasgow.

Brennan, J. and McGeevor, P. (1990) *Ethnic Minorities and the Graduate Labour Market*, CRE, London.

Cohen, L. (1989) 'Ignorance, not hostility: student teachers' perceptions of ethnic minorities in Britain' in G.K. Verma, *Education for All: A Landmark in Pluralism*, Falmer, Brighton.

Collier, J. and Burke, A. (1986) 'Racial and sexual discrimination in the selection of students for London medical schools', *Medical Education*, vol. 20, no. 2, pp. 86–90.

CRE (1987) *Learning in Terror. A Survey of Racial Harassment in Schools*, CRE, London.

CRE (1988a) *Ethnic Minority School Teachers. A Supplementary Survey of Eight Local Education Authorities*, CRE, London.

CRE (1988b) *Formal Investigation Report, St George's Medical School*, CRE, London.

CRE (1989a) *Evidence Submitted to the Education, Science and Arts Committee of the House of Commons – The Supply of Teachers for the 1990's*, CRE, London.

CRE (1989b) *Words or Deeds? A Review of Equal Opportunities Policies in Higher Education*, CRE, London.

DES (1989a) *Initial Teacher Training: Approval of Courses*, Circular No. 24/89, HMSO, London.

DES (1989b) *Responses to Ethnic Diversity in Teacher Training*, Circular 117/89, HMSO, London.

Giles, R. and Cherrington, D. (1981) *Multicultural Education in the UK: A Survey of Courses and Other Provisions in British Institutions of Higher Education*, CRE, London.

Gupta, Y. (1977) 'The educational and vocational aspirations of Asian immigrant and English school leavers: a comparative study', *British Journal of Sociology*, vol. 28, no. 2. pp. 185–98.

Kitwood, T. and Borrell, C. (1980) 'The significance of schooling for an ethnic minority', *Oxford Review of Education*, vol. 6, no. 3, pp. 241– 53.

Mac an Ghaill, M. (1988) *Young, Gifted and Black*, Open University Press, Milton Keynes.

MacDonald, I., Bhanani, T., Khan, L. and John, G. (1989) *Murder in the Playground*, Longsight Press, London.

Menter, I. (1989) 'Teaching practice stasis: racism, sexism and school experience in initial teacher education', *British Journal of Sociology of Education*, vol. 10, no. 4, pp. 459–73.

Milner, D. (1983) *Children and Race: Ten Years On*, Ward Lock Educational, London.

Morrison, A. and McIntyre, D. (1976) *Teachers and Teaching*, Penguin, Harmondsworth.

Singh, R. (1988) *Asian and White Perceptions of the Teaching Profession*, Bradford and Ilkley Community College, Bradford.

Siraj-Blatchford, I. (1991) 'A study of black students' perceptions of racism in initial teacher education', *British Educational Research Journal*, vol. 17, no. 1, pp. 35–50.

Swann, Lord (1985) *Education for All; Report of the Committee of Inquiry into the Education of Children from Ethnic Minority Groups*, HMSO, London.

Tomlinson, S. (l983) 'Black women in higher education: case studies of university women in Britain' in L. Barton and S. Walker (eds), *Race, Class and Education*, Croom Helm, London.

Tomlinson, S. (1986) *Ethnic Minority Achievement and Equality of Opportunity*, University of Nottingham School of Education, Nottingham.

Troyna, B. (ed.) (1987) *Racial Inequality in Education*, Tavistock, London.

University of London (1988) *Opportunity for All*, Conference Report, Institute of Education.

Wright, C. (1987) 'Black students – white teachers' in B. Troyna (ed.), *Racial Inequality in Education*, Tavistock, London, pp. 109–21.

CHAPTER 4

Equal Opportunities, Teacher Education and Europe

PAM BOULTON and JOHN COLDRON

This chapter provides an introduction to major pan-European activities over recent years on gender and teacher education. It considers issues of terminology and communication between co-workers and the influence of the differing contexts in which they work. It outlines the background and status of major initiatives including key legislation and funded projects. Some key themes are identified, and in conclusion consideration is given to what Britain can learn from, and what it can contribute to, work in this field.

It is impossible in the space provided to give a comprehensive overview of equal opportunities work across Europe; it is, therefore, important to establish the parameters of this chapter. It restricts itself to a discussion of work which has evolved from a cross-European origin, and involves European co-operation and networks. Sadly, it is also confined to a western European perspective and consequently says nothing about eastern European work. This is understandable with European Community initiatives, but it is also true that organizations such as the Association for Teacher Education in Europe (ATEE), although not restricted to membership from EC countries, has, at present, very little communication and representation from the former communist block countries.

The issue of language

In the drive for co-operation and mutual understanding on equal opportunities across Europe, terminology, conceptual understanding, and different tongues are important considerations. The terminology of equal opportunities in Britain is notoriously contentious. At its most damaging, the choice of terms and the meanings attached to them by individuals are used by some to categorize opinion and attitudes – what Ann Dummett (1992) calls 'the use of terms as an ideological test'. For instance, to choose the term 'equal opportunities' is sometimes taken to indicate a limited understanding of what are seen as issues of structural injustice. The users of this term may have their ideas and opinions dismissed as a consequence. A rigid insistence on 'correctness' of language can create a barrier to sympathetic and genuine discourse within Britain. In a wider context, with differing first languages, the problem is exacerbated.

This chapter has used the term 'equal opportunities' in its title, yet it will primarily deal with issues of gender. British readers may feel misled, yet this is perfectly appropriate for an analysis of the European context. In most of Europe, the term 'equal opportunities' applies to gender rather than a variety of sites of systematic disadvantage. Similarly, a number of different terms will be used to mean the same thing and the same term is used to mean different things. Thus what might be termed 'gender equality' is often referred to as 'emancipation', 'non-sexism' or, more frequently, 'equal opportunities'. 'Race' issues become 'migrant' issues, or 'alien rights' or 'Foreigners' Law'.

The clarification of terminology is but the first stage of understanding. From there we have to examine the ideological associations we may be assuming as we try to interpret important connotations of the meaning. Our understanding is likely to be rooted in the British context. It is important to stress how differing educational and societal structures can affect equal opportunities issues and the strategies adopted for dealing with them. This means that the attachment of positive and negative connotations to certain terms is unwise until the terminology is clarified, and there is understanding of the significance of those terms in the specific context of each country. For example, in considering progressive and reactionary forces at play in Irish education, reference may be made to the strength of the influence of trade unions in opposing government policies. British colleagues may misunderstand the debate if they do not realize that in Ireland the unions are perceived as reactionary and the central government Department of Education as progressive concerning equality of opportunity.

Finally, a discussion on terminological usage and understanding could not omit reference to different tongues. The examples of European co-operation cited here have relied predominantly on the use of English. Conferences and seminars use French and sometimes German, but never to a great extent. It would therefore seem that those from Britain have a distinct advantage. However, there are two sides to this coin. It is possible that those for whom English is a first language are more prone to make mistaken assumptions, whereas those who frequently speak in languages other than their own may be more aware of the need to clarify terms and concepts. If we are really to achieve meaningful dialogue, then we need continually to clarify the terms we use, and appreciate different perceptions determined by differing cultural contexts.

European co-operative initiatives

In an analysis of European co-operation on equal opportunities in teacher education, three influential strands emerge. They are the influence of the European Commission (EC), the ATEE, and the Nordic Council. Their work is, to a certain extent, inter-related and interdependent.

Although it might be argued that it has been slow to respond, EC policy has undoubtedly been influenced by the world-wide impact of the women's movement. As a cross-national organization, the EC may have felt an obligation to respond to the UN recommendations on Women's Decade, and international conferences in Mexico (1975), Copenhagen (1980), and Nairobi (1985). One factor that emerges when examining the origins of EC involvement in equal opportunities is that it is economic interests that provide the impetus for change. The emphasis throughout has been on enhancing career prospects for girls and boys so that girls can fill the projected shortfall in the technological labour market. There is evidence for this in the proposals and documentation of most of the equal opportunities projects supported by the EC. For instance, the handbook produced as the first initiative of the EC action programme launched in June 1985 said in its introduction: 'If young women are to play an equal role in a technology-based economy in the future, they will need to be nurtured into a technological culture early in their school careers' (European Commission 1985a). Demographic trends and forecasts of labour shortages are the driving force of the initiatives that have emerged over the last eight years. The focus is on subject choice as it influences career choice, sex-stereotyping as it constrains employment options, and career counselling.

The identification of demographic trends and economic need as the major determinants of change may be disconcerting for some. Economic trends have a habit of reversing. Women have the experience of two world wars in which their labour was needed and they operated as valued members of the workforce only to have these 'opportunities' removed as men returned to reclaim 'their' jobs. As demographic trends shift, will women once again become expendable?

However, as with many initiatives, the possibilities of extending and even subverting the original aims and intentions have been realized. When examining projects it is the breadth of approach and the width of interpretation of the brief that is most striking. The implementation of projects has moved far beyond issues of career choice. There are few areas that come within the remit of gender issues in education that have not been addressed. This 'subversion' is not the result of a conspiracy. It is inevitable that any initiative which deals with equal opportunities will be unable to address one particular thread in isolation. The factors which interrelate to produce a phenomenon such as sex-stereotyped career choice make a complex web. To address the issue is to address those other issues which relate to it. The personnel involved in these initiatives understand this. It is, therefore, important to look beyond the stated aims and intentions of much of the work and examine the ideas and practices resulting from project implementation.

The Treaty of Rome in 1958 made no direct reference to education in any context, although it did refer to vocational training. Moves to extend the influence of the then European Economic

Community into education were resisted by some member states in the 1960s and 1970s. The first major EC commitment to action in the field of equal opportunities and education was the Resolution adopted by the Council of Ministers for Education on 3 June 1985 (85/C 166/01). The Resolution required member states to implement a range of policies and action programmes, including one on equal opportunities for girls and boys in education. For the first time teacher education and equal opportunities were prioritized. One of the elements of the action programme was the question and pedagogics of equal opportunities in teachers' initial and in-service education (European Commission 1985b).

This Resolution led to the initiation of a Medium-Term Programme to fund projects and activities which included those relating to teacher education. The needs of the labour market determined the focus. When examining the implications of trends which would influence the completion of the internal market in 1992, the Commission prioritized the need to identify and extend action aimed at ensuring equal opportunities for girls and young women in education so as to encourage them to consider a full range of choices for training and employment.

On 31 May 1990, the Council and Ministers of Education agreed a Conclusion on the enhanced treatment of equality of educational opportunity for girls and boys in the initial and in-service education of teachers (90/C 162/05). The Council reaffirmed its commitment to the objective of achieving equality of opportunity for girls and boys in education, and saw the nature and quality of initial and in-service education of teachers as a major factor in achieving that objective. For instance, regarding teacher education curricula, 'authorities should . . . examine . . . how this question [equality of educational opportunity] could, to a greater extent, permeate the initial and in-service training of teachers . . . The training of teacher trainers . . . on issues related to equality of educational opportunity should be a priority area' (European Commission 1990).

For those in Britain, it is worth noting that the criteria for competence as defined in the proposals for school-based secondary teacher education (DES 1992) would seem to be in direct contravention of this Conclusion, to which the British Secretary of State for Education was a signatory. A further statement in the same document is also worthy of attention. It reads: 'the Council and Ministers recognise that the extent to which educational systems effectively deal with issues of equality of opportunity is an important indicator of the quality of the systems themselves' (European Commission 1990). This emphasis on the need to make commitment to equal opportunities a criterion of good teaching is the basis for much of the work in Europe. It is part of a philosophy which views the promotion of equal opportunities as the professional duty of every teacher and is linked with a dominant theme in European projects – the integration of equal opportunities in curricula.

The vehicle for much of the work of the action programme of the EC which operated from 1988 to 1991 was the ATEE (Arnesen 1991). This organization, established in 1976, was the first European forum for teacher education. Its work informed the 1985 EC Resolution, and it was no coincidence that the same year saw the establishment within ATEE of Standing Working Group 10 on Equal Opportunities for Girls and Boys in Teacher Education. As an organization which encompassed more than the EC countries, there was a strong Nordic influence in its work.

One of the most important and influential projects undertaken by Working Group 10, and funded by the EC, was the production of a European *Curriculum Framework for Teacher Education* (Arnesen and Ni Charthaigh 1987). The document was produced by a group of six people from Norway, Ireland, Portugal and the Netherlands. In many ways it is a seminal work. The framework is a comprehensive outline of appropriate curricula for both pre-service and in-service teacher education.

The curriculum framework was an important factor in the initiation of a cycle of activity by the Commission which began with the 1985 Resolution. This cycle involved the identification of key areas for development, the setting up of pilot projects based on an action research model, their implementation and evaluation and finally a stage of dissemination. The pilot projects were realized as the Teacher Education Network (TENET) Project. Led by an Irish European Co-ordinator, it lasted from 1988 to 1991, and comprised thirty-five projects in eleven EC countries. TENET was aimed at integrating equal opportunities in the curriculum of teacher education.

It is perhaps surprising that Britain contributed via initially two, and then only one project. Why was participation so meagre from a country which has contributed so strongly to feminist and educational debate and which has an Equal Opportunities Commission which monitors equal opportunities legislation? A number of causes suggest themselves. Was it a result of central government hostility which at best engenders minimal compliance with EC activity? Did it reflect a context in which our educational bureaucracy at all levels consistently failed to prioritize equal opportunities as an issue? Was it the result of a feeling among those with expertise in Britain that they were further advanced than their continental colleagues on these issues, and therefore had little to learn? Was it simply a case of poor communication where those who might have put forward proposals were never informed about the programme? Whatever the causes, opportunities to gain valuable funding for action research, to establish networks, and to influence work in Europe have been missed. European Commission initiatives still lack significant British participation and influence.

The third important influence in pan-European work is the Nordic countries and their Council. While some Scandinavian countries were excluded from TENET, as non-EC members, their contribution to European co-operative networks has been strong. The Nordic Council of Ministers has an Equal Opportunities Committee. A Nordic Project, similar to TENET and lasting from 1992 to 1994, has recently been approved under the direction of a Norwegian co-ordinator (Arnesen 1991). Again, the emphasis is on teacher education. The project aims to stimulate the development of an equal opportunities perspective in the content and methods of teacher education; to develop a Nordic network in the field of equal opportunities in teacher education; and to support bilateral exchange between institutions and countries.

Different contexts for educational change

A European perspective provides greater understanding of the cultural and material conditions within which people work. The promotion of equality of opportunity in education is approached in broadly similar ways because similar concerns are shared across Europe. These concerns are both pragmatic and based on principle. Pragmatically, the need for a viable pool of labour has led to the pressure exerted at all levels to encourage women to be more ready to make non-traditional career choices. As a matter of principle there is a demand for justice from women in each country supported by the international women's movement. Patriarchy is a fact of European culture. It is the privileged position of men over women in all areas of social importance – governmental, managerial, legal and administrative. For all of the supposed and real differences between European nations this aspect of life is a common heritage. Primogeniture, the identification of women with the domestic, the denial of education and intellectual status – all of these, and many more, are shared European experiences. With few exceptions, such as childcare provision, they lead to similar manifestations of inequality – few women in positions of influence, sexual oppression, rigid distinctions of male and female characteristics and unequal treatment in the education system.

Each country has ostensibly similar systems of teacher education (Eurydice 1991). However, there are significant differences. These stem from the variety of educational cultures within which the systems operate and the differing histories of education and teacher education in each country.

The idea that educational cultures can differ should not be a very difficult thing for a British audience to grasp since we have undergone, in a relatively short space of time, a transformation of our educational ethos. From a culture of schooling, characterized by a relative degree of professional autonomy and respect based on the paradigm of care, we have moved to a culture where the teacher is alienated and the paradigm for educational relationships is the marketplace (Apple 1983).

Britain is not the only European country to have experienced significant change over a short period. The Portuguese revolution was a profound turning point in all sectors of Portuguese life. The process to democratize society that was begun in April 1974, ushered in enormous changes in legislation. Since that date it has been a principle enshrined in the constitution that there should be equality between the sexes. It is compulsory for this to be explicitly integrated in all legislation. A focus, therefore, of work on gender in Portugal is to try to bring the actual culture of families and schools into line with the explicit legitimation provided by powerful legislation (Palma and Marques 1992).

The effect on education, and therefore on teacher education, of the commitment to democratic processes is fairly recent in Portugal. In Denmark, however, the ideal of democracy has been a central principle for many years and this has led to a system explicitly designed to achieve this ideal. It is argued that if children are, when they become adult, required to participate in a democratic society then they need to learn how to do so. Further, it is recognized that schools are especially important communities within the democratic state. They should be models of democracy and be managed on exemplary democratic principles. Anything else would be both hypocritical and threaten the democratic process itself. This approach permeates the whole of the education system and is as much a vital part of teacher education as of schooling. A major practical consequence is the requirement to negotiate the curriculum with pupils at all levels. Clause 16 of the Danish 1975 Education Act states: 'The detailed planning and organisation of teaching, including the choice of teaching style, methods and content, shall to the greatest possible extent be a co-operative venture between teacher and pupils.' Pupils are encouraged to co-operate with others, to take responsibility for their decisions and to have an influence on their own development. The teacher is allowed considerable freedom in the use of the national curriculum and in choice of teaching methods (Boysen 1992).

To an English audience this participative process may seem highly progressive and exceptionally well suited to allow the requirements of students at all levels of the system to have their needs acknowledged and met. Indeed, the provision in Denmark of 93 per cent childcare for three- to four-year-olds would seem to support this. It is salutary, therefore, to note that the problems of equality for women and girls in Danish society closely parallel those in Portugal and England.

In Denmark, too many girls are quiet and self-effacing in the classroom, boys more demanding; more women are out of work and/or relatively poorly qualified; in the teaching profession (and therefore in teacher education institutions) a disproportionate number of women teach the younger children and more men teach the older classes and are subject teachers (Cain 1990).

In Portugal, the media propagate stereotypical images of men and women; women account for 63.4 per cent of the total unemployed; women account for only 16.8 per cent of higher administrative posts; women teachers are concentrated in the early years of schooling but male headteachers predominate to a ratio of 40 per cent to 60 per cent; only 31 per cent of teachers in higher education are women; girls are much quieter and self-effacing (Palma and Marques 1992).

While a Portuguese colleague might use the legitimation of an imposed legal requirement as the argument for change, a colleague in Denmark may call on people to live up to the shared axioms of a national culture. If the movement for the promotion of equality is subtly different in different contexts then so also is the working of patriarchy. The end product of patriarchy, namely oppression, and the consequent necessity for resistance are, however, the same whatever the context. What changes is the way that patriarchy and resistance position themselves within the discourses that constitute social life in general and educational discourse in particular.

The discourse is influenced not only by the particular manifestations of sexism and patriarchy but also by the national history of each country. In Ireland, for example, the status of education and teachers is markedly different from that in England because it has been affected by Ireland's recent colonial past: 'what happens in schools has tremendous significance for all classes and strata in Irish society in the absence of other distributable forms of wealth . . . to enter the labour market at any level requires credentials' (Lynch 1989). The powerful role played by the Catholic Church is also a crucial aspect of education in Ireland. The power enjoyed by this single religious institution is in direct contrast to the careful balance of power maintained between Protestant and Catholic in the Netherlands where there is a constitutional requirement to balance any provision between the two. In Ireland the promotion of equality of opportunity enjoys the strong support of government departments and, as has been noted elsewhere in this chapter, Ireland has been in the forefront of European initiatives on this issue. The Department of Education has issued brochures promoting the cause of gender equality in the classroom and has supported a large-scale curriculum development project in Irish primary schools focused specifically on gender (Lavin and McHugh 1992).

This strong governmental support is in the context of a culture that arguably has reactionary policies on abortion, contraception and divorce. The specific patterns of teacher education designed to fulfil the demands of this society will necessarily be complex. As noted earlier in this chapter, it is important to rid one's mind of stereotypes when attempting to gain a multinational perspective.

Historically, countries like Spain, England, Portugal and France have trained secondary teachers through a more academically demanding university structure while primary teachers have been trained in less prestigious colleges of education. In most European countries there is a move to ensure that primary teachers are trained to the same standard and that all teachers are graduates (Blondel 1991; Eurydice 1991; Morgenstern de Finkel 1991). Britain has been at the forefront of this trend, aiming for an all-graduate profession since the 1970s. It is interesting to note that in Britain the gradual loss of status of teachers has been accompanied by a relegation of the need for institution-based education.

It is precisely these realizations, born out of contact with European colleagues, that can illuminate the position in Britain. It encourages pertinent questions. Although constitutionally democratic, do we have a democratic culture to call upon? Does comparison with the Danish context cast doubt on this? When people pay lip-service to equality of opportunity in education what principles do they invoke – egalitarian or pragmatic? How far is our equal opportunities legislation imposed on a hostile or indifferent population in our schools and teacher education institutions?

Benefits and contributions

This section identifies four major themes. They are the concept of integration, varying curriculum models for teacher education, the competing claims for cognitive and affective approaches, and the question of legitimacy.

One of the terms used frequently in European initiatives is 'integration'. The TENET programme, for example, focused on the integration of equal opportunities in the curriculum of teacher education and the Nordic project refers to 'the development of curricula that have equal status and sex role perspectives both as an integrated part and as individual projects' (Nordic Proposal 1989). Integration in this context means that gender equality is not merely a discrete add-on element, but a necessary, substantial and explicit ingredient of the education of teachers. This means to incorporate equality, to make it an indivisible part of being a teacher. Equality issues pervade every aspect of the teacher education curriculum. Integration is permeation in the best sense of the term.

The attempt to go beyond permeation signals dissatisfaction with the permeation model. Experience in Britain has rightly induced cynicism towards the concept and its effectiveness. But what is wrong with a model that calls for equality issues to pervade the curriculum? Does the perceived inadequacy of the model refer to problems of implementation, or to the hijacking of the model by the complacent and those with vested interests in homoeostasis?

There is no doubt that in practice the adoption of a permeation model means that some tutors can pay lip-service to equality in their courses. If disillusion with permeation is justified, is the stress on integration misconceived? In our opinion this is not the case but if integration or permeation is to be reinstated as an ideal it is necessary to identify the various factors which damage the effectiveness of the approach. In this way the features necessary to enable permeation to succeed can be identified. We need a stronger and clearer characterization of what is needed to implement the ideal in practice. The European and Nordic networks and the many action research projects undertaken throughout Europe are an invaluable resource for this.

The curriculum of teacher education in Britain is likely to be influenced strongly by competency-based approaches. Criticisms thus far have focused on the inadequacies of such a skills-based approach. It is feasible that a precise and comprehensive curriculum for teacher education, designed by teacher educators, will be the most appropriate response to the current competency proposals. Many other European countries have a more prescribed curriculum, although the prescription has not always emanated from central government. A common theme in all countries is that of change via the medium of curriculum innovation and there is a wealth of examples and experience in the designing of curricula for teacher education that explicitly incorporates the promotion of equality of opportunity. There are models that are based on themes (similar to those in CATE 24/89), on disciplines (such as philosophy, psychology and sociology) and on school curriculum subjects.

A further theme which has been a feature of pan-European debate, is a familiar one. It concerns the promotion of attitudinal change, and the conflicting emphases of cognitive and affective approaches. Initiatives which have used a curriculum intervention model tend to consider cognitive approaches as significant. However, it is also true that initiatives have often combined these approaches. The question of the effectiveness of cognitive approaches in teacher education raises significant practical and theoretical issues. The implementation of work with different emphases in varying contexts is a valuable resource and merits further investigation (Arnesen 1992).

An issue of great importance for anyone wishing to promote change is the legitimacy that can be claimed for those changes. Legitimacy can be conferred by, for example, legislation, European or national initiatives, funding and through government or institutional policies. Coming from 'above', these are empowering. Legitimacy can also be provided by our immediate context – our peers, colleagues and members of the research community and the milieu in which we work. Being from those around us and on our 'level', this is emotionally and intellectually supportive.

Each country has a different 'mix' of such horizontal and vertical support. A striking aspect of the British scene is an exceptional level of activity at the 'grass roots'. For example, there is a tradition of experimental and student-centred learning that forms an influential part of British education theory and practice which is well established in teacher education departments. This tradition is necessarily open to arguments concerning equality, justice and the welfare of students. It also contributes a great deal to the development of an alternative practice of teacher education that emphasizes process as well as content and the construction rather than the transmission of knowledge. While it is possible to find similar approaches and traditions in other parts of Europe, Britain is distinctive in the level of research and the range of teaching materials available for use in school classrooms and teacher education institutions. All of this is a valuable resource and should be seen as an important contribution by Britain within the wider context of Europe. Examples of other influences on the milieu in which we work are the following. An influential body of publications has been published in English and has had a considerable impact on the practice of teacher education. The Equal Opportunities Commission has supported and initiated important work in this area. Most local education authorities, especially (but not exclusively) those responsible for urban schools, produced policies and practical support for the promotion of equality in schools and teacher education institutions. While recent changes have rendered some of these policies impotent, resources – both human and material – remain.

For some of those countries which possess a written constitution equality is, in various ways, explicitly stated as a tenet of the state. Britain does not have such a constitution, but appears nevertheless to have comparatively good support from 'above' in the form of legislation, the Equal Opportunities Council, and innumerable institutional policies. However there is little doubt that this has been very much weakened by the ethos of the Conservative government since 1979 which has, under the influence of the 'new right', made clear its opposition to an emphasis on equality issues in teacher education. This equivocal support is further weakened by the virtual dismantling of the power of LEAs and the fragmentation and overloading of the education service since 1988. A considerable benefit offered by European involvement is the legitimacy conferred by the European Commission that can serve to provide the empowerment denied by our national government.

We have much to gain from and much to give to European colleagues. We are all facing similar problems stemming from a common heritage and shared material conditions. The specific contexts are different enough to make fruitful comparisons and so to illuminate our own concerns. Such contact offers powerful legitimation and, most importantly, a network that offers practical, intellectual and emotional support from many times more colleagues than we have in Britain.

References

Apple, M. (1983) 'Work, class and teaching' in S. Walker and L. Barton (eds), *Gender, Class and Education*, Falmer, Lewes.

Arnesen, A. and Ni Charthaigh, D. (eds) (1987) *Equal Opportunities for Girls and Boys. A Curriculum Framework for Teacher Education with guidelines for Action*, Report to the Commission of the European Communities, Brussels.

Arnesen, A. (1991) 'Equal opportunities in teacher education – a European perspective', unpublished Conference Paper, Madrid.

Arnesen, A. (1992) 'Knowledge and consciousness raising' in P. Boulton, L. Cohen, J. Coldron and H. Povey (eds), *Ways and Meanings: Process, Gender, and Teacher Education*, Pavic, Sheffield.

Blondel, D. (1991) 'A new type of teacher training in France: the Instituts Universitaires de Formation de Maîtres', *European Journal of Education*, vol. 26, no. 3.

Boysen, L. (1992) 'Democratic teaching processes and equal opportunity' in P. Boulton, L. Cohen, J. Coldron and H. Povey (eds), *Ways and Meanings: Process, Gender and Teacher Education*, Pavic, Sheffield.

Cain, M. (1990) EQUOP: Esbjerg Seminarium TENET Equal Opportunities Project – Report of Second Phase Esbjerg Seminarium.

DES (1992) *Reform of Initial Teacher Training: A Consultation Document*, 28 January.

Dummett, A. (1992) 'Problems of translation', *The Runnymede Bulletin*, no. 252, February.

European Commission (1985a) *Action Handbook – How to Implement Gender Equality*. Stationery Office, Dublin.

European Commission (1985b) Resolution of the Council and Ministers for Education. 85/C 166/01, Brussels.

European Commission (1990) Conclusion of the Council and Ministers of Education on the Enhanced Treatment of Equality of Educational Opportunities for Girls and Boys. 90/C 162/05, Brussels.

Eurydice Unit (1991) *Initial Teacher Training in the Member States of the European Community*, Eurydice Unit, Brussels.

Lavin, P. and McHugh, H. (1992) 'Empowering primary teachers' in P. Boulton, L. Cohen, J. Coldron and H. Povey (eds), *Ways and Meanings: Gender, Process and Teacher Education*, Pavic, Sheffield.

Lynch, K. (1989) *The Hidden Curriculum: Reproduction in Education, An Appraisal*, Falmer, Lewes.

Morgenstern de Finkel, S. (1991) 'The slow reform of teacher education in Spain', *European Journal of Education*, vol. 26, no. 3.

Palma, A. and Marques, R. (1992) 'School links with families for the promotion of non-sexist education' in P. Boulton, L. Cohen, J. Coldron and H. Povey (eds), *Ways and Meanings: Gender, Process and Teacher Education*, Pavic, Sheffield.

Black and Female Student Experience

CHAPTER 5

Issues and Concerns for Black Women Teachers in Training

MAUD BLAIR and UVANNEY MAYLOR

In this chapter we examine the experiences and perceptions of black[1] women student teachers in one College of Higher Education. Fairways College (the name of the College and that of the students has been changed to maintain anonymity) is situated in a multi-ethnic town in the South of England. At the time of the study, which was done in 1991, twenty-four out of the 661 students in the college were from black ethnic minority groups. There was one black assistant researcher with a six hours per week teaching brief. The data presented here were collected from recorded life-history interviews of eighteen women (ten African-Caribbean and eight South Asian), spread between the first and final years of the primary or secondary BEd degree and the PGCE. Of the twenty-four black students, four women declined to take part in the study, and two were males. The decision to exclude both males and white women was a deliberate one as the aim of the study was to use the life-history method to explore the specifically gendered and racialized experiences of black women. The project[2] therefore, deliberately set out 'to make explicit a black female point of view' (Essed 1991). There were, in any case, only two black male student teachers at the time of the research, a situation which, we would argue, itself requires critical analysis. The perspectives of white women teachers, on the other hand, are well documented (see, for example, Acker 1983; ILEA 1984, 1987; McLaren 1985; De Lyon and Widdowson Migniuolo 1989; Coffey and Acker 1991). While we cannot claim that the policies and practices and the experiences of the black students in one College of Higher Education are representative of other teacher education courses, our study nevertheless adds to the scarce data available on the subject of black students in teacher education (see Bradford and Ilkley College Conference 1991; and Siraj-Blatchford 1991).

We begin with a brief discussion of some of the reasons why these women chose teaching as a career and outline some of their major concerns about their experiences of teacher education. We therefore present our observations of the overall aims and objectives of Fairways College and assess the effectiveness of the College's policy and its implications in the light of students' own accounts. We also look at the strategies used by black students to deal with the situations in which they found themselves, and their continuing attempts to influence change within the College. Finally, we make some suggestions for an approach to teacher education which takes account of difference and of differential educational experiences, and which we hope will contribute to more effective preparation of potential teachers for teaching in the diverse and unpredictable world of the school and the classroom.

Teaching as a career for black women

> For as far back as I can remember, I have always wanted to be a teacher (believe it or not)! Having achieved this, I sometimes wonder why. To be honest, I did have some idealistic notions of individually contributing towards 'changing' aspects of the education system. (Bangar and McDermott 1989, p. 137)

Existing evidence suggests that young black people consider racism to be the most significant deterrent to their becoming teachers. They are concerned about the low status of black teachers and their marginalization into support services, in particular Section 11.[3] They share with their white peers a concern about the problems of discipline, low salaries and low promotion opportunities, but see skin colour as a significant determining factor for black teachers. They are particularly concerned about the racism of white pupils and teachers against black teachers (Singh 1988). As a general rule, black teachers continue to feel undervalued, their skills unacknowledged, their careers stunted and their contribution marginalized. The evidence also indicates that it is generally black teachers who are burdened with the responsibility for the multi-cultural curriculum (Banger and MacDermott 1989; Bhattacharya 1990; NUT 1990; Bradford and Ilkley Community College 1991; Rhakit 1991). Some feel that they are given the most difficult classes, which, it is felt, inhibits their career prospects (Sethi 1990). One result of such observations is that few black young people choose teaching as a career (CRE 1988; NUT 1990). What, then, motivated the women in our study to enter teaching?

Black women have many and varied reasons for choosing teaching as a career, or for becoming teachers. Some were, like Bangar above, driven by idealistic motives or a desire to be the role models they felt that they had themselves not had. Others made choices according to specific circumstances at specific moments in their lives. One student had enjoyed her work experience during the fourth year when she had worked in a nursery. Another had spent time teaching English to adult learners and had been encouraged by her students and colleagues to take up teaching as a career. For others, teaching was something they had always wanted to do for as long as they could remember. Others *became* teachers because their choices were constrained by family commitments or cultural expectations. For Yasmin, going to college would postpone the possibility of an early marriage, and teaching would enable her, when the time was right, to do a rewarding job while fulfilling her domestic responsibilities. There was as much variety of cultural experience within as between different cultural groups. Some students of different South Asian origin were able to pursue their choice of career without any obstacles while others had had to negotiate and compromise with family anxieties about leaving home. Yasmin observed that Muslim women were generally disproportionately underrepresented in degree courses. But while it might be tempting to explain this absence primarily in terms of religion restricting Muslim women's choices, Yasmin felt it was the weight of *patriarchy* which operated in *different* ways across cultures and this could not be restricted to women of South Asian origin (see also Brah 1992).[4] As Yasmin states:

> If it had been a boy instead of me, he would have been allowed to go to London or wherever he wanted to. But being a girl, parents are stricter in these areas.

Statements such as this, we would argue, can be heard in a wide range of situational and cultural contexts. Not all students were by any means keen to leave their home environment, neither was the pressure which they experienced necessarily always from the home. One South Asian student who had chosen to live in the hostel with other students felt that she was under pressure to join in extra-curricular activities which she did not particularly enjoy. As she put it, spending her evenings in the pub was not her idea of fun. She had also had to resort to getting her food from the canteen when the food she prepared for herself had begun to 'disappear' from the communal refrigerator in the hostel. Within a term, she had gone back to live at home.

All the mature students with children had chosen the local college and gone into teaching either because they were now ready to pursue a career which they had wanted but had hitherto not been able to pursue for a variety of reasons, or because their family commitments left them no choice. There were, therefore, many different and interconnecting factors which determined student choices of teaching as a career and of location of college, but gender emerged as the single most important *constraining* factor in these choices. For some students, being a woman, a wife, or a mother had significantly influenced their career options and/or the location of the college. It did not, however, necessarily influence their perceptions of their own identities.

> I can't say I've ever made a decision because I'm black or a woman. They are decisions that I wanted to make. Although they are both important to me, i.e. being black and female, they are not as important as getting what I want and getting where I want, hopefully. I'm just me, an individual. (Sonia)

> I see myself as an individual . . . I don't know if it has to do with the philosophy course that I did, but we have arguments at home about it. They tell me, 'but you are so and so'. I say I'm an individual first before I am a mother, a wife, a daughter. I am myself . . . Sometimes when we talk amongst Asian people I sometimes have to keep quiet because I feel like I dare not say anything because I'm the odd one out in these thoughts. (Sahena)

One of the advantages of the life-history interview lies in the opportunity it provides to view the range of factors that come together to influence and shape an individual's life. Whatever the weight of the specific forms of external pressure, it was clear that these women *negotiated* and retained an independent space for themselves, albeit sometimes at some cost, as Sahena shows.

Black women in college

The black women interviewed for this study had a number of concerns which were personal, domestic, religious and/or cultural. Some issues, however, exerted greater pressure so that during interviews, students were inclined to focus on such issues and obscure or underplay the complex interaction of a range of influences on their lives. However, we would agree with Mac-Mahon (1991, p. 33) that 'the subjective sphere is the means through which we make sense of ourselves, to ourselves and to the world'. We therefore selected those issues which the women themselves identified as being of greatest concern to them. For example, we found that gender played a major part in their choice of career. Once at college, however, the experience of being black students within a predominantly white college raised overwhelming concerns about racism which overrode their concerns over any other single issue and went beyond *individual* experiences to unite the different categories of black women in specific ways. For example, they were conscious of and concerned about sexist practices which disadvantaged women.

> They said the course caters for mature students yet they don't cater for children. We start at 9 a.m. and finish at 5 p.m. Often it is difficult for women with nursery and school age children to be there for 9 a.m. . . . and it means having someone to collect the children. Some can't afford to pay for this. When you come for an interview, you are not told that you might finish at 5 p.m. because they want you to come. Also, we used to get half term, like the schools, now we don't. That means you have to make alternative arrangements. If you're a single parent this is difficult. (Muna)

> Some of the lecturers had the attitude that I had not got my priorities right, having children and then going back to college. Lectures start at a quarter to nine and I had to take my son to nursery school first, drop my daughter off at school and get myself to college for a quarter to nine . . . I asked if I could be a little late, and he said, 'That's fine', and then when I did actually turn up 2 or 3 minutes late, he said, 'you can't come in. You have

to go away, you can't just barge in'. . . . He wouldn't listen when
I told him I had already asked his permission. (Naomi)

But it was their experiences of racism within the college which
they most wanted to talk about. Racism, they felt, affected their
relationships with white students and their interactions with lecturers and aroused acute anxieties about their chances of success.
Regardless of individual levels of political consciousness, all the
students were conscious of the importance of skin colour in
white constructions and assumptions of 'race'. The sense of being
differentially positioned *vis-à-vis* white women, and white people generally, as well as the sense of themselves as a numerical
minority, gave these women of diverse linguistic, cultural and
geographical origin a sense of solidarity, an example of which
they demonstrated in a collaborative theatrical production
about their experiences in the college.

Multicultural/antiracist policies[5]

How was the issue of racism taken up and dealt with in the college? There is every indication that much time and effort was
invested in the production of the Multicultural Policy at Fairways College. The Policy acknowledges the role of the College
in the life of the community. It underlines the effects of racism
on the life chances of black people. It aims for a curriculum
which is opposed to racism and which takes account of the multi-
cultural nature of British society. It exhorts all members of the
College to observe the Policy and to promote a positive environment for all its members. But, however admirable a statement it
may be, it appears to have got caught in a cul-de-sac of its own
good intentions. Without guidelines and a forum for regular
reflection it cannot be properly implemented, without commitment and leadership it cannot be enforced, and without an
understanding of its meaning and importance it can encourage
resentment or simply be ignored. The basic weakness of such
policies lies in their failure to engage with the complex nature of
individuals and with the structural and ideological aspects of
institutions (Jewson and Mason 1992). Those who are entrusted
with implementing them, members of staff within the institution,
are unable to relate to the issues addressed by such policies, for
reasons which we shall show. There is, therefore, little incentive

to accord status to such a policy and no basis upon which to monitor its effectiveness.

Student perceptions

Racism, as experienced by the students who took part in the study, ranged from well-meaning but often patronizing and clumsy attempts to acknowledge cultural differences to blatant expressions of bigotry. Some of them, particularly those who had come to Britain as adults, often rationalized hurtful situations by referring to their relative unimportance (a general comment, for example), or by the fact that the person had not meant any harm, or they viewed such events as products of prejudice or ignorance which they were able to ignore. That such events were frequent and hurtful was nevertheless apparent. This is not to say that overall these students had unhappy and totally demoralizing experiences. They had formed cross-cultural friendships and appreciated that some lecturers were able to accept differences and to treat *all* their students as individuals and not attempt to impose ethnic identities on them. Those women who had been educated in British schools had come to teaching with a strong belief that they could be role models and could do something to reduce the disadvantages in terms of experiences and academic achievement of black pupils in schools. They actively attempted to influence the curriculum by suggesting topics or contributing materials which added to its range and diversity. They also challenged some of the assumptions about black people which filtered through the curriculum and through their relationships with lecturers and students. Some of them were, however, surprised to find that despite an environment in which problems of discipline were not an issue, where class could be overlooked as a determinant of achievement, and 'cultural attitudes to education' (Foster 1990) were clearly not a consideration, the assumptions and stereotypes normally associated with black children in schools were nevertheless also to be found at the level of teacher education. For example, one second-year African-Caribbean student who had a record of good assignments, whose first language was English, who could not speak Creole and did not speak any other language or dialect at home, was suddenly deemed to have 'a language problem' when one of her assignments was not of the usual standard. The lecturer's assumption that Creole interfered with the student's ability to express herself in English may have been motivated by concern to consider all the factors which might affect his student. But the association of 'language problem' with being black in spite of the fact that the student had successfully passed A-level English and her first year BA, has implications for the kind of assumptions which lecturers may hold when marking assignments written by black students. The tutor's intentions may have been to help the student, and not to undermine her. The effect, however, was to anger the student and to destroy her trust in her tutor, whom she felt had low expectations of her.

Policies and their effects

It is not surprising, in our view, that policy statements on multi-cultural/anti-racist education should find a resting place in the deep recesses of an official's draw. What is missing from such policies is an understanding of the inherently contradictory nature particularly of those relationships between white lec-turers/teachers and black students which are underpinned by 'good intentions' or 'tolerance'. Many individuals would not recognize themselves in the type of person which such policies appear to address. Most individuals, and indeed most institu-tions, would project themselves as having a caring and profes-sional approach towards their students (Bagley 1992). The case of the African-Caribbean student which we described may be just such an example. Unless the complexity of different forms of racism is addressed (Rattansi 1992) and the interplay between 'race', gender and class (MacDonald *et al.* 1989) is understood, a great deal of the time and (often emotional) energy which goes into the production of such policies will be wasted. A statement made by one student commenting on the kind of advice given to students about preparing topic work in primary school, serves to illustrate the need for a more complex understanding of individual subjectivities.

> We were doing things about the Victorians and then we started talking about if you were in class you say to your children, 'bring something from home about the Victorians'. I think well hold on,

> my parents were brought up in the West Indies and they would have nothing Victorian about them. If my children were in school now, they would have nothing Victorian . . . They would put children at a disadvantage. Black children, not only West Indian but Asian because they couldn't, I mean things like photographs. (Jean)

It would seem that this lecturer's approach was as much a feature of class as it was of her ethnocentricism. The type of task that student teachers were being asked to store up for future use could have excluded a range of pupils who could not have fulfilled the teacher's request. Many working-class children and white children from poor families would be unlikely to possess valued Victorian artefacts. It is clear that teachers would need more than sensitivity to cultural differences or to children's original geographical and cultural origins in order to involve all children fully and equally in the class activity. It would, therefore, have been necessary to encourage students to bear in mind alternative but relevant tasks in addition to requests for Victorian artefacts. To focus on racism or ethnocentrism alone would be to ignore a range of ways in which the lecturer could be undereducating her students. Another example was provided by Muna.

> We had to write an assignment on a scientist and he gave us a list of examples of people that we could study and towards the end of the lesson he said, 'Oh by the way, don't forget, because we've got to be looking at multi-cultural things all the while, don't forget there are lots of non-white people who have created lots of good inventions'. But he wasn't able to give an example, so he didn't encourage anybody to do it.

Here, the lecturer's lack of commitment to searching for anti-racist materials and his deliberate neglect of information relating to black scientists may have been a factor of his ineffectiveness so that it is probably safe to conclude that he was unlikely also to have made the effort to find examples of women scientists (black and white), many of whom remain invisible in the canon of scientists studied in schools and colleges. Thus racism and sexism combine to deprive students of a broad-based understanding of science and to limit their teaching skills. His deliberate singling out of black scientists may have constituted, for him, an adequate attempt to implement the College's policy to 'teach with a perspective which has a world view rather than an ethnocentric one'. But instead, it could have reinforced the racist notion, particularly in students already operating with a racial frame of reference, that there were no black scientists to speak of and that those that did exist were not worth the effort of study.

The black teacher as 'professional ethnic'

Another insidious practice, which occurred in the College as well as during teaching practice in schools, was that of regarding black teachers as 'professional ethnics' rather than as teachers with a broad range of talent and knowledge to offer. That is, it was assumed that black students possessed specialized knowledge and expertise of minority ethnic cultures and customs, a practice which can lead to the marginalization of black teachers and endanger their chances of promotion (Bangar and McDermott 1989).

> It's like, because I'm Asian I should know everything multi-ethnic. I don't. I remember when we were doing something in relation to Diwali, I was asked to do a quick summary of it and I did. I thought fair enough, but then afterward I thought about it. Why should I have done it, why couldn't somebody white look into it? (Gita)

Gita rightly concludes that all teachers should be encouraged to take an interest in and develop an understanding of the subject regardless of perceived cultural affiliation. This point was forcefully brought home to Gita while on teaching practice.

> We were exploring food with the class and the teacher said, it was just the way she said, 'Oh *you* can do all those foreign things'.

On another occasion,

> She [the teacher] said, 'I think you had better speak to her seeing as how you are the same colour, she'd probably listen to you'. So I said, 'but I don't even speak the same language. We may be the same colour but our cultures are different'. I have to do this explaining every time I encounter something like 'you are the same'.

It could be argued, of course, that the teacher genuinely felt that, given the context in which black children feel excluded, this child may have related better to someone her own colour, regardless of culture. It does, however, raise the question about what the teacher would have done had Gita not been present, and what message this gives to all the children in the class. For Gita, who may have misunderstood the teacher's intentions, this was nevertheless one of numerous examples of being assigned the status of 'professional ethnic' in the school as well as at College and the tendency to assume that categories such as 'Asian', or African-Caribbean are internally homogenous.

But while, on the one hand, black students were most 'visible' when 'race' or ethnicity was discussed, some lecturers professed and practised colour-blindness in two ways. The first was to negate the identity of the student.

> A general comment which didn't respond to but which I thought about recently was, 'Well, I don't see you as Asian, I just see you as . . .'. And I thought it's an odd thing to say, but I put it aside and didn't think about it. But when I thought about it, I thought what a stupid thing to say, how can you not see me as Asian. I am. (Neena)

Ironically, statements like this are often made out of a sense of politeness – a wish to express tolerance, to make difference seem unimportant and to make the other person feel accepted. There is usually a lack of awareness of the inherently hierarchical relationship that such a statement establishes. The contradiction and tension between some forms of politeness/tolerance and racial/cultural inferiorization are not understood and seldom taken into account in discussions about policy.

A second but different example of colour-blindness was recounted by Maureen.

> If you have an answer and you put up your hand the lecturer will look past you and look at another student and if they've got their hand up, then they will ask that person. And still if it's a wrong answer they will ask somebody else and they will take a long time to get to you. So it's sort of they're just trying to cut you out. They ignore you as a person to answer the question. They probably don't think you've got the right answer.

It is interesting that Maureen does not say that the lecturer dislikes black students but that she or he does not expect the black students to have the correct answers. While it is not possible to draw general conclusions from this statement without further exploration of the conscious or unconscious forces at play, it illustrates what we have found to be a general sense of insecurity among students about lecturers' attitudes towards their work and their potential as teachers. It is also consistent with some existing accounts of interactions between teachers and black pupils in schools. (Wright 1987; 1992). This sense of vulnerability among the students was particularly evident during teaching practice.

> I picked up immediately from the class teacher that she didn't have high expectations of me at all. I thought, my tutor is writing all these nice things about me, but when it came to the crunch the result I got was rather disappointing. I thought I was doing really well, but she was colluding with the teacher. She wasn't listening to me at all, she just took the teacher's view completely. (Lucille)

This acute awareness by black students that partnership/collusion between their tutor and their placement school did not necessarily work in their favour and that 'race' was often a determining factor, must raise questions about the proposed system of mentoring.[6] How much support are they likely to get from their tutor if the mentor is racist towards them? How much sensitivity will be employed in assigning mentors to black students? To what extent do black students keep quiet about racism for fear that they will be marked down? Students do worry that when they report white children's racist behaviour, it is taken as an inability to maintain control (Bradford and Ilkley Community College 1991). We would argue that the majority of student mentors are unlikely to be deliberate racists. But how much understanding will they have of the possibility that their own sense of 'tolerance' or of 'professionalism' could blind them to their own negative assumptions which could undermine the interests of black students? Who is to provide children with an understanding of the need for respect for *difference and diversity* when teachers are themselves at times guilty of fostering disrespect among the pupils? One mature student gave this account of her experience of teaching practice.

> She [the class teacher] was always harping on about the fact that I was a trainee . . . I pointed out to her that I was not going into school for the first time, I had been teaching for eight years and I am a qualified teacher, and that I am doing the course because I need the DES recognition . . . But it didn't matter what I was

> doing she would say, 'No, you don't', and she wasn't respecting
> me in front of the children. That's what was wrong, she wasn't
> giving me the respect that was due. (Sahena)

Although examples of blatant expressions of racism were few,
the feeling by black students that they were often singled out for
different and generally negative treatment was consistent across
the cohort.

> We were talking about presenting maths to infant school children
> and the lecturer said that if they don't understand a particular
> thing you call them a 'silly nig nog'. And she sort of looked at the
> group and she said, 'Oh, I'm not meant to use that word, am I?
> You just call them a silly idiot', and she laughed it off. (Levine)

Teacher educators who would actively encourage such forms of
racism among their students are probably in a small minority. In
any case, most white students do not blindly replicate such
behaviour. But it does raise the serious question about what is
done about teacher educators who actively encourage teachers
to abuse children, whatever that form of abuse might be. How
much understanding of racist abuse and harassment is there
among teachers and what do teacher education institutions and
schools do to create this understanding? The attitudes of some
of the white students illustrate the extent to which they shared
certain representations and understandings about 'race' with
their lecturers, as Michelle found out:

> The second year I was at college, I was living in one of the blocks
> and I went to take a bath. I went into the bathroom and I heard
> one of the girls say,' I bet she needs to scrub herself with a Brillo
> pad to get herself clean'. Another time I was doing my hair and
> they asked me, 'Do you wash your hair the same way we do?'

Forms of resistance

Despite their own experiences, the women in the study were
more concerned about the impact that racism had on black
pupils and felt strongly the need to challenge stereotypes within
the College. During a discussion about the banana trade, for
example, the lecturer turned to the black student and suggested
that she was the best person to tell the group about bananas. The
student's response was, 'We don't actually grow any bananas in

Croydon'. On another occasion the black students collaborated on a play which exposed many of the subtle forms of racism which they experienced in the College. The genuine horror that many of the white students felt on learning that such things happened in the College suggested that the issue had barely touched their consciousness. Black students, on the other hand, routinely confronted racism which was either directed at an individual, was expressed through inference or innuendo, or was directed at black peoples generally. Yet even on those occasions when white students witnessed the more extreme forms of racism, it was left to the black students to do the challenging or to express disapproval. This may have been due to the sense of powerlessness that white students themselves felt about challenging lecturers. This meant of course, that black students were the more likely to be seen as trouble-makers. On other occasions the tacit collusion of the white students with racism left black students feeling isolated and publicly humiliated. Nadia, who was training to be a PE teacher but for whom swimming was not a particularly strong area, described a situation when the tutor invited her to have a practice session at a time when she had been led to believe that the swimming pool was empty. She arrived to find all the other students present but that she was going to be the only one swimming. The tutor explained this by saying that it was a way of helping Nadia develop self-confidence. It had the opposite effect, and left Nadia feeling that the tutor had deliberately set out to make a fool of her. This had not been the first occasion when the tutor had singled her out. White students had also recognized this and sympathized with Nadia. Although Nadia persevered, she had seriously considered giving up the course a number of times.

Conclusion

While we would not deny the importance of encouraging as many black people as possible into the teaching profession, we consider that the often *exclusive* focus on recruitment to be short-sighted, if not at times counter-productive. It is equally important, in our view, that teacher educators address those issues which serve as obstacles to young and mature entrants to teaching. In order to do this, teacher educators will need to examine the steps being taken to equip teachers with the skills they need to teach in a dynamic and complex society. Students should recognize that individual identities are complex and multi-dimensional and that therefore they cannot be pigeon-holed into assumed cultural categories. While different forms of racism need to be identified, it is, however, equally important to recognize that however different the nature of specific forms of racism may be, the emotional impact on the recipient does not necessarily depend on the type of racism encountered, and does not leave the individual with time to grade emotions according to the perpetrator's level of intention or understanding. Teachers particularly need to understand this if they are properly to support their pupils' emotional needs.

All tutors and mentors need to be sensitive to all their students. Where white tutors and mentors are assigned to black students, it is important to bear in mind the possible ambivalence in the tutor/mentor's relationship with the student. This might mean, for example, that the tutor/mentor genuinely wishes to foster the interests of the student, yet employs racial criteria in assessing the student's work.

We would endorse the need for policies which serve to *guide* members of the institution in those responsibilities which they do not necessarily take for granted and whose importance is not necessarily accepted by all. However, to be effective, such policies would need to be reviewed regularly in order to engage with people's levels of understanding of the issues in question. There needs to be proper understanding of the meaning of multi-cultural/anti-racist policies. It is also important to engage with the different ways in which people locate themselves in relation to the issues addressed by such policies. We are thinking here in particular about the conflict between good intentions and effects. It is necessary also for policies to address the complex interplay between issues such as 'race', gender, class and so forth and to allow individuals the space to examine the assumptions which inform their thinking. Policies should be collaborative and should be written in such a way that they empower people rather than foster a feeling of defensiveness.

We would recommend that discussion forums for different groups are created in order to enable students to come together with others who share their concerns and can communicate them to a senior manager who has responsibility for equal opportunities. This point was made particularly forcefully by black student teachers at a conference on teacher education (Bradford and Ilkley Community College 1991).[7] They felt that such groups could help overcome feelings of isolation among students but that, unless they were approved by the college, they were likely to be regarded as pressure groups and the students labelled trouble-makers. Another advantage of such groups would be the ability to form links with students in other colleges.

We recommend that teacher education institutions examine the nature of their partnerships with schools. Students are not always prepared for the kinds of experience they meet in school (Menter 1989; Tickle 1991). But while black teachers can also expect to face the types of traumas which most teachers face and have to learn to cope with their emotions where the decisions they make might affect children's welfare, we would argue that black teachers should not have to 'cope' with racism. Close collaboration is, therefore, necessary between the college and the placement schools in order to ensure full support for students. This would involve the need to communicate clearly to schools the values and expectations of the college. The kinds of concern which we have outlined should be discussed with the head of the school and students should feel able to talk about these concerns and know that s/he is taken seriously. Sometimes student links with tutors during teaching practice are very limited, while the nature of the communication between the tutor and the head of the school is an unknown factor to the student (Bradford and Ilkley College 1991). Open communication, both oral and written, between the head of the school, the tutor and the student is particularly important to black students who, like all students, depend on the headteacher for a report but who may fear that an assessment of their competence may be based on their ability to 'cope' with racism. We also recommend a clear set of procedures to follow where a placement raises concern.

Finally, we would conclude that black student experiences (like those of any other students) are complex and not confined to racism. However, a denial of racism or resistance to deal with this problem denies black students the right to a fulfilling experience of teaching, can lead to student drop-out, discourages potential black teachers from entering the profession, and is wasteful of the valuable talents that black teachers bring with them to the teaching profession.

Notes

1 We use the term 'black' to refer to all students of African-Caribbean and South Asian origin.
2 The interviews were carried out by Uvanney Maylor as part of a doctoral thesis on black women in teacher education.
3 This refers to the special DES funding arrangements made under Section 11 of the 1966 Local Government Act, for the educational needs of 'ethnic minority' children.
4 Brah maintains that while South Asian women share common experiences as *black women*, different categories of Asian women have different concerns and different problems which relate to factors such as migration and class and which are compounded by patriarchal racism within the British state.
5 We refer to these policies in this way in order to show that a gap existed between policy and practice regardless whether the policy was multi-cultural or anti-racist.
6 At the time of writing, having mentors for student teachers is not yet universal practice.
7 We are grateful to Ranjit Arora for making the report of this conference available to us.

References

Acker, S. (1983) 'Women and teaching: a semi-detached sociology of a semi profession' in S. Walker and L. Barton (eds), *Gender, Class and Education*, Falmer Press, Lewes.

Bagley, C.A. (1992) 'Inservice provision and teacher resistance' in D. Gill, B. Mayor and M. Blair (eds), *Racism and Education: Structures and Strategies*, Sage, London.

Bangar, S. and McDermott, J. (1989) 'Black women speak' in H. De Lyon and F. Widdowson Migniuolo (eds), *Women Teachers: Issues and Experiences*, Open University Press, Milton Keynes.

Bhattacharya, R. (1990) 'The position of black teachers today', unpublished paper for the Holland Park and West London Black Teachers Groups.

Bradford and Ilkley Community College (1991) *Ethnic Minorities and Teacher Education*. Conference Report.

Brah, A. (1992) 'Women of South Asian origin in Britain: issues and concerns' in P. Braham, A. Rattansi and R. Skellington (eds), *Racism and Antiracism: Inequalities, Opportunities and Policies*, Sage Publications, London.

Coffey, A, and Acker, S. (1991) ' "Girlies on the warpath": addressing gender in initial teacher education', *Gender and Education*, vol. 3, no. 3, pp. 249–61.

CRE (1988) *Ethnic Minority School Teachers: A Supplementary Survey of Eight Local Education Authorities*, CRE, London.

De Lyon, H. and Widdowson Migniuolo, F. (eds) (1989) *Women Teachers: Issues and Experiences*, Open University Press, Milton Keynes.

Essed, P. (1991) *Understanding Everyday Racism: An Interdisciplinary Theory*, Sage Publications, London.

Foster, P. (1990) *Policy and Practice in Multicultural Education*, Routledge, London.

ILEA (Inner London Education Authority) (1984) *Women's Careers in Teaching: a Survey of Teachers' Views*. Research and Statistics Report.

ILEA (1987) *Women's Careers in Secondary and Primary Teaching: The Birmingham Study*. Research and Statistics Report.

Jewson, N. and Mason, D. (1992) 'The theory and practice of equal opportunities policies: liberal and radical approaches' in P. Brahan, A. Rattansi and R. Skellington (eds), *Racism and Antiracism: Inequalities, Opportunities and Policies*, Sage, London.

McLaren, A.J. (1985) *Ambitions and Realizations: Women in Adult Education*, Peter Owen, London.

MacDonald, I., Bhaunani, T., Khan, L. and John, G. (1989) *Murder in the Playground*, Longsight Press, London.

MacMahon, M. (1991) 'Nursing histories: reviving life in abandoned selves', *Feminist Review*, no. 37, pp. 23–7.

Menter, I. (1989) 'Teaching practice stasis: racism, sexism and school experience in initial teacher education', *British Journal of Sociology of Education*, vol. 10, no. 4, pp. 459–73.

NUT (1990) *Memorandum of the Executive of Black Teachers*.

Rattansi, A. (1992) 'Changing the subject? Racism, culture and education' in J. Donald and A. Rattansi, *'Race', Culture and Difference*, Sage Publications, London.

Rhakit, A. (1991) 'Black teachers' lives and careers', unpublished MA dissertation, Warwick University.

Sethi, A. (1990) 'Black teachers', unpublished paper, Holland Park and West London Black Teachers Groups.

Sikes, P. and Troyna, B. (1991) 'True stories: a case study in the use of life history in initial education', *Educational Review*, vol. 43, no. 1, pp. 3–16.

Singh, R. (1988) *Asian and White Perceptions of the Teaching Profession*, Bradford and Ilkley Community College.

Siraj-Blatchford, I. (1991) 'A study of black students' perceptions of racism in initial teacher education', *British Educational Research Journal*, vol. 17, no. 1, pp. 35–50.

Tickle, L. (1991) 'New teachers and the emotions of learning teaching', *Cambridge Journal of Education*, vol. 21, no. 3, pp. 319–28.

Wright, C. (1987) 'Black students – white teachers' in B. Troyna (ed.), *Racial Inequality in Education*, Tavistock, London.

Wright, C. (1992) 'Early education: multiracial primary school class-rooms' in D. Gill *et al.* (eds), *Racism and Education: Structures and Strategies*, Sage Publications, London.

CHAPTER 6

One of the Boys? Gender Identities in Physical Education Initial Teacher Education

ANNE FLINTOFF

Introduction

Despite a wide range of feminist research,[1] arguably one of the most central gaps in our understanding of the ways in which gender inequalities are reproduced through and within education is the role of initial teacher education (ITE). To what extent does the ITE curriculum help students to understand the influence of gender as a continuing and major determinant of educational achievement, but also, to what extent does the *process* of ITE itself, reflect and reproduce gender (and race) inequalities? As Leonard (1989, pp. 27–8) notes, 'colleges . . . [both] have theories about education *and* are practical institutions . . . The issue is . . . *what* is taught and learned and *how* it is taught (in the sense of the broadest social relations within which learning takes place) in universities and polys.' This chapter focuses on the ITE of intending secondary PE teachers, and critically examines the way in which male and female students negotiate and construct their gender identities within one particular ITE institution.[2] Physical Education (PE), as a specific subject area, is of importance to debates about gender relations not just because of its strongly gendered, single-sex, historical development in Britain (see, for example, Fletcher 1984), but also because of its close links with the body and physicality on which common-sense ideas about gender difference and inequality rely. Scraton's work (1985; 1992; forthcoming) has been important in highlighting the negative implications for girls of moves towards co-educational PE at school level, yet the implications of co-educational PE ITE, compulsory practice for some years as a result of the introduction of the 1976 European Law of Equal Treatment, has yet to be explored.[3]

This chapter draws on data gathered as part of a larger study of the initial teacher education of intending secondary PE teachers in Britain, which aimed to critically examine the relationship between PE ITE and the reproduction of dominant images of masculinity and femininity and gender-appropriate behaviour.[4] Rather than focus on the details of the formal curriculum *per se*, documented elsewhere (see Flintoff, forthcoming), this chapter critically examines the broader social relations operating within one PE ITE institution. The main part of the research included a term's observation in two case-study institutions involved in the initial training of PE teachers, together with semi-structured interviews with key decision-makers such as the course leaders and heads of departments. The two case-study institutions were chosen to reflect the separate and distinct historical development of the subject and are typical of those currently involved in the training of secondary PE teachers. One, which I have called Heydonfield, had been a former men's college of PE, and the other, which I have called Brickhill, and from which the data used in this chapter are drawn, had been a former women's college of PE, and is now part of an institute of higher education. Since there were very few black students on the ITE courses at the institution and only one black member of staff, the data presented in this chapter provide insights into the experiences of white PE students and staff.[5]

I have chosen to concentrate in this chapter on data collected from Brickhill because of its unusual gender profile. Unlike the majority of teacher education departments, the gender profile of staff and students within Brickhill's PE department was skewed in favour of women, reflecting its history as a former women's PE college. This context had implications not only for the actual content and organization of the teaching (see Flintoff, forthcoming) but also, as this chapter describes, for the way in which gender identities were negotiated and constructed within the institution.

A note on theoretical issues

Despite an emphasis in much recent feminist work in education on practical ideas and strategies (see, for example, Whyte *et al.* 1985; Burchell and Millman 1989), theoretical explanations of the process by which gender relations are reproduced have developed and moved beyond the earlier, too simplistic, and now widely criticized, 'sex role' stereotyping theory (see, for example, Connell 1987; Walby 1990). As well as ignoring the power differentials between male and female sex roles, the idea of *a* sex role which people 'acquire' unproblematically, denies the diversity of behaviour *within* 'masculinity' or 'femininity', and fails to capture the way in which these behaviours vary between different cultures, classes, or over time, as well as how individuals may challenge and resist such stereotypes. Some more recent and adequate accounts have recognized how class, as well as 'race', intersects with gender to shape both pupils' educational experiences and achievements (Arnot 1982; Brah and Minhas 1985; Amos and Parmar 1987) as well as their teachers' lives, work and careers (Acker 1989; De Lyon and Widdowson Migniuolo 1989).

A more promising account of gender identities and roles is given by Brittan (1989), who argues that sex-role theories are too simplistic and fail to recognize the *politics* of gender formation. Gender, he suggests, should be seen as having no fixed form, as something which is never static and which is always subject to redefinition and renegotiation. Gender is an accomplishment – something which has to be worked at in every social situation, and something which is always tentative. However, each social situation does not evoke a potentially new gender identity. He argues that in modern Western society, at least, the way in which people accomplish gender in more or less the same way is guaranteed by the naturalness of heterosexuality, by the central belief that biological differences are central to sexual and gender behaviour. This ensures that there *are*, then, certain characteristics associated with femininity or masculinity which strongly reinforce expectations of appropriate behaviour for boys and girls, men and women, and which are reproduced in and through the practices and policies of institutions, including schools. The diversity of behaviours is not random. Some characteristics become culturally dominant, and accepted as 'natural', while other kinds of behaviour are defined as deviant or inferior in relation to these. While it is important to stress that the dominant images of masculinity and femininity are not the most *common* patterns of behaviour – 'not many men or boys really are the strong, cool, fit, competent macho types who populate cigarette ads', as Kessler *et al.* (1987) put it – most men, and women, *are* directly affected and influenced by these gendered images and stereotypes.

It is the nature of the relationship between these two sets of attributes and behaviours which is central to an understanding of gender. Culturally accepted notions of masculinity and femininity do not exist as simply *different* but are constructed in a hierarchical relationship to each another. It is *masculine* values, behaviours and attitudes which are valued more highly than feminine ones. Moreover, masculinity and masculine values have become defined in direct opposition to femininity and feminine values – being masculine involves a *rejection* of the feminine. However, although masculinity is always constructed in relation to, and superior to, femininity, it is too simplistic to talk of *one* masculinity. Gender relations rely on the creation of hierarchies *within* gender categories, as well as *between* gender categories (Connell 1987). Dominant forms of masculinity – which Connell (1987) has called 'hegemonic masculinity' – exist in relation to subordinated forms of masculinities, as well as to femininities. While the reproduction of dominant masculinity may involve the use of physical force, hegemony is achieved largely through consent, through the work of gender ideologies. Gender ideologies serve to conceal the power differentials between the sexes, so that male domination becomes accepted as legitimate, as the 'natural' way for society to be organized. Gender ideologies are reproduced and sustained through the practices of institutions, including, for example, the media and education. However, hegemony always has to be struggled for, it is never won once and for all, but has to be worked for. For individual men, Brittan (1989) argues that masculinity has to be worked at. It can never be accepted as a 'finished product' but has to be *accomplished* in a permanent process of struggle and confirmation – a process he has called 'identity work' – and although masculinity carries with it a lot of privileges and power, there has been more recently a recognition of its costs in contemporary society, including, for example, the suppression of emotion (see, for example Mapp 1982). In terms of femininity, while, there are different forms of femininity, Connell (1987) argues that the lack of social power held by women as a group means that the organization of a dominant form of femininity over others, operating in the same way in which hegemonic forms of masculinity suppress subordinated femininities, is less evident. Instead, he suggests that 'emphasised' femininity, a form of (heterosexual) femininity 'organised as an adaption to men's power, has become the accepted, and within a patriarchal society, the *ascribed* form of femininity' (Arnot 1984).

Gender relations, then, have to be seen as a constantly changing, shifting set of relationships, based on negotiation and contestation, a process in which some groups clearly have less resources and power.

The role of educational institutions in this gendering process is a complex one, but Kessler *et al.* (1987) suggest that schools are involved in arbitrating between different kinds of masculinity and femininity, providing the context for one kind or another to become dominant or hegemonic. This organization of ideas about masculinity and femininity – what Kessler *et al.* (1987) call a school's 'gender regime' – is constructed not only within and through the formal aspects of the institution (the content, organization and pedagogy of the curriculum and school policies) but also through the more hidden aspects of school life, such as the informal peer-group life of pupils, or the relationships between teachers and pupils.

Brickhill – a feminine gender regime?

Given its history as a former women's PE college, the strong emphasis within the curriculum on 'feminine' PE activities such as dance and rhythmical gymnastics and its still heavily-skewed student intake, the research was particularly interested in the way in which male students responded to working within such a 'feminine' gender regime. Although there is a considerable amount of feminist research detailing the nature of classroom interaction and behaviour of boys at school, very little of this has been at higher education level. For example, Askew and Ross's (1989) research found that there was an almost constant 'power play' underlying the interactions between boys – an ongoing process of positioning and a continual seeking of status and prestige. Boys not only related to activities competitively, but competition seemed to be the primary source of their motivation. This operates, they suggest, both explicitly in terms of the way in which it permeates social interaction in the classroom, and implicitly in the ways in which they approached different activities. Did similar kinds of behaviour characterize classroom interaction at Brickhill? A term's observation of PE classes at Brickhill showed that a great deal of male students' behaviour did revolve around 'doing' such masculine 'identity work' and engaging in such competitive power play.

Competition, aggression and physicality in the social construction of masculinity

As Connell (1987) has noted, body sense is crucial to the development of male identity; to learn to be a man is 'to learn to project a physical presence that speaks of latent power'. Sport and physical activity provide an important *context* for men to learn not only how to use their bodies to produce such effects, but also to experience 'the combination of skill and force in powerful, dominating ways'. It also provides a context for men to *demonstrate* and display their physicality publicly, as well as to test this in relation to other men.

> The social definition of men as holders of power is translated not only into mental body images and fantasies, but into muscle tensions, posture, the feel and texture of the body. This is one of the ways in which the power of men becomes 'naturalised'. (Connell 1987, p. 85)

Despite this, it is important to note that relatively few men do actually embody such characteristics or choose to become actively involved in sport – in this sense, PE students (both male and female) are quite atypical.

Many of the practical PE sessions at Brickhill provided the ideal context for male students to display aspects of 'hegemonic' masculinity, particularly games such as rugby or football which had been introduced into the curriculum at Brickhill specifically 'for the men'. These men-only sessions were always noisy, physical and competitive, with student involvement and effort at a maximum. On the few occasions when the group stopped to discuss an issue, the fidgeting and 'fooling around' which ensued made for a quick return to practical work. As one lecturer noted, the competitive game situation was a 'good means of motivating the group'. Men who were not particularly able in the game tried even harder to get 'involved', even though it was clear that some were far from happy with the physical violence of the game. As Jackson (1990) notes, there is huge pressure for men to conform to the accepted codes and values of hegemonic masculinity and try to become 'one of the boys', even if they do not agree with much of what is going on.

Although I was obviously restricted by my sex to only observing formally constituted male-only settings within the curriculum such as the rugby sessions, it is likely that other male-only contexts at Brickhill (for example, the male changing rooms, the 'initiation' ceremonies for incoming male students, or the after-match 'socializing' after weekend games) served as other important 'spaces' for the reinforcement of hegemonic masculinity. Other research has shown how the mocking of women and homosexuals, both of whom are seen as a threat to the traditional image of what it is to be a 'man', is central to rugby club and male locker-room cultures (see, for example Dunning 1973; Curry 1991). These are areas of research where much remains to be done, and would seem appropriate contexts for men wishing to research and work within the area of gender and sport/PE.

In other invasions games sessions (that is, games where the primary aim of the game is to invade the opponent's territory, as in basketball, or soccer, for example), taught on a co-educational basis, the effects of the competitive and aggressive behaviour by male students were particularly noticeable. Even in those games, such as hockey, where the majority of women were more experienced than the men, a central core of male students, empowered by their physical presence and size, dominated the play. In one PGCE soccer lesson, the final 'game' was dominated by three male students who spent most of the time running the ball through groups of less talented students to score as many goals as possible. Since students were only involved in limited discussions within the formal curriculum about the ways in which gender affects classroom interactions (see Flintoff, forthcoming), it was not at all surprising to observe that lecturers did not intervene or challenge such interactions in their *own* classrooms. In fact, when I asked staff if the presence of male students made any difference to their practical sessions, most felt that the men contributed *positively* to groups – 'they really stretch the rest', 'they're more lively and competitive' and 'they are an addition' were typical comments.

Women and homosexuals as 'other' in the social construction of masculinity

An alternate 'identity-building' strategy to the use of direct physical contests with other men was the use of verbal 'put-downs'. One of the most common insults used to put down or trivialize other men's performances was to suggest that they were performing like a 'real nancy' or like a 'girlie' (a derogatory term used by male students to describe women PE students).[6] As Messner (1987) notes, masculinity is defined in terms of what it is not – that is, not feminine and not homosexual. While this abuse has the effect of putting down particular men (men who did not match the ideal of hegemonic masculinity) the overall effect is to disparage *all* women.

Using women and homosexuals as negative reference groups (Stanworth 1983) meant that male students distanced themselves from any behaviour or activity associated with femininity. Unlike the application and effort they showed in games, many male students went out of their way to demonstrate their *lack* of commitment to 'feminine' activities like dance. Laughing, 'fooling around', exaggerating their lack of skill, or wandering around the room and interrupting other groups, served as other signals to each other, the lecturer, and the female students, that they were not taking the activity seriously.

Since to touch other men in any other way but aggressively may result in their heterosexuality being questioned, it was not surprising to note that it was in activities such as dance, or gymnastics, which involved students in touching, lifting or supporting one another, that there were the most examples of male students' unease, and homophobic comments and gestures (see Flintoff 1991). Comments such as 'Ooh, honey, don't touch me there' or 'Lovely, do that again!' were common expressions used by male students to cover their embarrassment. These acted to reinforce the display of appropriate 'gendered' behaviour by male and female students, but also to make virtually untenable the position of any student (or member of staff) whose sexual orientation is not heterosexual.

It is important to mention that there *were* a few male students who were actively involved in dance, since they illustrate how individuals can and do successfully negotiate a gender identity outside the 'accepted' image of masculinity, and how this is never the same or straightforward process for each individual.

A third strategy of masculine identity work was to use the women students as a negative reference group. Throughout the fieldwork, I was struck by the way in which many of the male students exuded confidence in themselves and their own abilities, and how many of the women seemed to lack confidence and underestimate their abilities for what appeared to be no good reason. There was little evidence of male students reflecting critically on their individual performance or progress, whereas the women, if anything, tended to underestimate or be too critical of their own performance, a tendency which characterizes many girls at school level, too (see Stanworth 1983). As Wood (1984) notes, the *outward* 'face' of masculinity is characterized by confidence, brashness, fluency and 'presence', even if the inward face is often the reverse.

In lots of very subtle ways, male students boosted their own confidence and status within the group by *diminishing* that of the women. One of the common methods of embarrassing a woman student, and at the same time doing a bit of 'body building' – Benyon (1989) uses this term to describe how boys would impress peers through acts of cheeky bravado against the staff, and it seems an appropriate term here, too – was for a man to shout out aloud in a full lecture hall that the woman sitting next to him had a question. Another was to groan loudly if a woman asked a question. Derogatory comments about their performances were common: 'typical woman' or 'just like a woman' were directed to women who made mistakes. It is important to note here that the women students involved did not always accept such put-downs passively. Some protested, although somewhat half-heartedly, others reacted more angrily, and some simply tried to carry on and ignore the comments. There is a real dilemma for women here, for as Mahony (1985) notes, if girls (or women) overtly challenge such situations, it may simply result in a redoubling of efforts to disrupt; on the other hand, to stay silent and to opt out of engagement can be viewed as a measure of male control of the situation. An alternative view, she suggests, is to see staying silent as a positive, self-chosen strategy of resistance.

Despite the undermining of women, there was also evidence to suggest that the men students *relied on* and *used* the women students for help and support in their work. For example, when students were set small-group tasks which involved one person acting as the chair and feeding back their ideas, a woman would invariably be pushed into this role. Collecting handouts or reading lists or finding out the times and locations of lectures were other examples of how women 'serviced' the men.

As well as putting down their performances within sessions, another important way in which women were controlled was through the explicit 'sexualizing' of situations at their expense. I am using the term in the same way as Halson (1989) does – to describe how male students deliberately introduce jokes and sexual innuendos into everyday classroom interactions. The centrality of the body in PE meant that there were numerous opportunities for the introduction of sexual innuendos, and for the sexualizing of particular contexts: for example, a partner stretch in gymnastics was suggested as a new sexual position, a progression for a flik flak involving thrusting the hips forward was a 'good exercise for later, lads', and a video of a young girl rolling in the gym provided an opportunity for female objectification by male students. Sexually appraising looks or gestures, often fleeting and very subtle, were also used. While these incidents might be dismissed as trivial, and may be less extreme than some described by others within school environments (Mahony 1985; 1989; Halson 1989), they serve none the less to reinforce the 'naturalness' of heterosexuality, and a construction of male sexuality based on objectification and conquest. These situations left women with little option but to 'go along' with the 'jokes', or risk being labelled as 'a spoilsport' – a situation commonly experienced by women in other settings (see, for example, Burgess 1989; Cunnison 1989).

I have focused on the male students' behaviour here because, despite being in the minority, there was a definite sense in which a small group of male students dominated the ethos of some of the sessions. As Wood (1984) has suggested, it is often difficult to convey through writing the way in which gender power relations structure situations without reducing boys (or men in this case) to one cultural grouping, and girls (or women) to another. Like him, what I am trying to suggest is that there were times when a group of men were 'dominant', and where their influence on the atmosphere and ethos of the group was great, whereas at other times the men and women students seemed to interact much more closely. But the ethos of sessions was also affected by the actions and behaviours of the lecturers, and although there is insufficient space here to detail examples, it is important to note that, on many occasions, it was some of the male lecturers who instigated a sexualized ethos within the sessions.

Being female in PE ITE

There is a danger that in focusing on the actions of male students and on the construction of masculinity within PE, female students and the ways in which they negotiate their own gender identities will be lost. The reproduction of an 'emphasized femininity' is not always without resistance or struggle. The fact that these women were physically talented, and had chosen a career within PE, already marks them out as women who have (at least to some extent) already successfully challenged existing patriarchal notions of women's physical capabilities (Leaman 1984). Dewar (1990) notes that for the majority of female students in PE, negotiating an identity with which they feel comfortable involves making sure, first and foremost, that they are recognized as heterosexual, feminine and attractive. For many of the women students at Brickhill, this appeared to be the case. Many of the women students, particularly in the early years of the undergraduate degree, took great care to emphasize their femininity and heterosexuality, for example through their dress and appearance and through the way in which they avoided particular 'masculine' activities. 'Feminizing' the PE 'uniform' included rolling up tracksuit bottoms to reveal very 'feminine' pastel-coloured ankle socks (very much in fashion at the time of the research) together with the wearing of make-up and heavy jewellery. However, not all of the women adapted their dress in this way. Many of the older students (in classes where there were very few male students at all) did not seem to have the same kinds of concern about their appearance, suggesting perhaps that the increased presence of male students was an important element in the younger students' moves to demonstrate and exaggerate their femininity.

There were times when some of the women were clearly uncomfortable with being 'female' in mixed settings in PE. I noted earlier how some of the PE contexts were sexualized by male students and staff at women's expense. The potential for this was increased in some sessions where women's bodies were most clearly on display, such as swimming or gymnastics. Informal conversations with the students confirmed that their choice of wearing long teeshirts over their swimming costumes until the last possible moment was an attempt to control the extent to which their bodies were 'on display'. Given the general lack of explicit recognition of sexuality within educational institutions generally (see, for example, Holly 1989; Kelly 1992), it is perhaps not surprising that issues of sexuality have been similarly ignored within the PE profession.[7] While mixed PE *could* offer a better experience for girls and women, as Scraton (1987) has noted, it could also simply increase the opportunities for men's objectification and gaze.

For the majority of women students, maintaining their heterosexual identity meant *avoiding* 'masculine' activities such as weight training or soccer, together with a distancing from the few women who were involved in such activities. The extra-curricular involvement of most of the women was in 'acceptable' women's sports such as netball, hockey and gymnastics. The few women who did participate in 'masculine' sports (there was, for example, a small group of strong soccer players) risked their heterosexuality being questioned – to quote one woman student, although she enjoyed learning soccer in the formal curriculum sessions, she would not get involved in the women's club because she viewed them as 'a bit suspect, if you know what I mean'. As Lenskyj (1987, pp. 384–5) notes, 'institutionalized compulsory heterosexuality still serves to constrain women's sporting participation: sports continue to be classified as feminine or masculine depending upon their function in enhancing heterosexual attractiveness'. The fact that many of the women accepted and used the name the 'girlies' themselves serves to illustrate the importance of heterosexual attractiveness in the construction of their own identities – they were prepared to collude with the use of the label, despite its other, objectionable characteristics.

Conclusions

This chapter has described the ways in which male and female students constructed gender identities within one particular PE ITE institution. It has focused specifically on male students because, although they were in the minority at Brickhill, their influence on the ethos and nature of the interactions within PE sessions was significant. The consequences of male students' gender 'identity' work for women students, and their experiences of their training, were immense. There is little evidence here to conclude that co-educational PE ITE at Brickhill has been a positive step forward for women, or that this form of organization is contributing to a diminishing of gender differentiation and inequality within the profession. Rather, PE classes seemed to provide a context for the exhibition of strongly gendered interactions between students, with 'feminine' activities and contributions from women students being devalued and undermined. If the move to a co-educational form of PE ITE is to fulfil its potential for challenging the restricted and limiting ideologies of femininity which characterized the former women's PE colleges, then several aspects of the current practice would need to be changed.

Challenging the nature of knowledge within PE ITE

There needs to be the development of a critical and questioning approach to the part PE ITE plays in the reproduction of gender relations. This will entail, among other things, a critical review of the kinds of knowledge included in courses, central to which is the selection, timetabling and teaching of practical activities. Co-educational PE ITE raises important questions for the profession regarding the nature, form and timetabling of practical activities for which there are no easy solutions. The discussion above has suggested that both single-sex timetabling of activities, and mixed groupings, present issues and problems which cannot simply be ignored, particularly in those activities which are most strongly 'gendered'. Co-educational groupings in PE classes also raises particular issues for teachers of Muslim students (whether at higher education or school level) who may object to such direct contact with males on cultural and moral grounds (see Carrington and Leaman 1986). Students need to be sensitized to the ways in which they can enable the full participation of *all* girls to take part in PE.

If the data collected in my research is representative of PE ITE more widely, it is likely that activities central to women's PE, such as dance, will be squeezed or eventually disappear. For ITE in PE to be effective in moves towards challenging gender inequalities it needs to strongly resist the slide towards a masculinist version of PE, and support a broad and balanced practical curriculum.[8] Teacher educators need to provide a lead in producing teachers who are prepared to teach across a range of activities, but also who have developed 'a critical consciousness about how and why PE takes on its current form and content, about which groups benefit from PE and which groups are empowered, and how PE can be used for emancipatory purposes' (McKay *et al.* 1990, p. 64). An ITE curriculum dominated by scientific, behavioural disciplines – increasingly the direction in which courses are moving (see Dewar 1990; McKay *et al.* 1990) – will do little to challenge students' performance-orientated perceptions of PE, or alter the ways in which they are able to sense of their own gendered identities within this.

The difficulties of raising gender issues as a professional issue – identities at stake?

Students need to recognize and be sensitive to the ways in which gender relations are reproduced not only through the formal aspects of a school's gender regime, but also through less formal aspects – through the everyday interactions between pupils and between pupils and teachers. They need, too, to be sensitized to the way in which the gender inequality is cut across and compounded by relations of class and 'race'. The presentation of this kind of material to students is often difficult and emotionally exhausting and, more often than not (if raised at all), is left to a small group of committed (usually female) staff, working in the professional studies elements of the courses, rather than seen as the responsibility of the whole staff team. Raising equality issues within subject studies is also crucial, since research suggests that this is one of the areas of their course which students see as most relevent (Denscombe 1982). Similarly, the promotion of equality must be central in the criteria by which students are assessed on teaching practice (see Equal Opportunities Commission 1989).

Given the central role of sport and physical activity in the reproduction of dominant forms of masculinity (Connell 1990; Whitson 1990), it is not surprising that some male PE students find the presentation of material which challenges such forms of masculinity personally threatening, and react by trying to disrupt sessions or discredit the material (see Sikes 1991). Sensitivity to its potentially personally threatening nature needs to be a careful consideration in the planning of such work with students.

Challenging gender relations within ITE

Work which directly addresses equality issues must continue – although, within the current changing scenario of teacher education, it is difficult to see how it can avoid being squeezed rather than extended (see Leonard 1989). However, without a wider acknowledgement by *all* lecturers and teacher mentors of the way in which gender relations are reproduced through the interactions in their own sessions, and more broadly within their institution, the hard-fought attempts by committed feminists to introduce students to knowledge which explains women's and girls' position within education and PE in terms of social relations and power, will remain largely ineffective. The power of the hidden curriculum and the informal culture of an institution's own gender regime has to be recognized and confronted. We need to work towards a position where the ethos of PE ITE is one in which male and female students feel able to display a range of behaviours, attitudes and values and not just those narrowly defined by dominant images of masculinity or femininity. This will not be an easy task, but will mean, in particular, questioning and challenging the ways in which male students assume the right to dominate the ethos of sessions as described in this chapter – by their competitive and aggressive behaviour towards one another, by putting down women, or by sexualizing situations at their expense.

To do this, lecturers will need to question their own practices – not only how they might encourage or even initiate such interactions, but also how they might be *differently positioned* to benefit from them and, more importantly, to counter and challenge them. Male teachers in school can, and frequently do, use their masculinity as well as their sexuality to control and motivate classes in ways not to open to their female colleagues (Benyon 1989; Holly 1989). The same is true for lecturers in ITE. As Griffin (1989) notes, a willingness to explore the effects of gender relations on our relationships and work as lecturers ourselves is necessary if we are effectively to address the same issues with our students. Without this, co-educational PE ITE in Britain will continue to represent what Walby (1990) has called 'an historical regress' in the position of women – where the position of women has *deteriorated* rather than advanced. Certainly, the gender regime at Brickhill described here shows how quickly a former women's PE college can become just another 'school for the boys' (Mahony 1985).

Notes

1 Although there are a number of feminist positions (radical, liberal, socialist, etc.), I am using the term in its broadest sense here to describe research which takes women's subordination to men as its starting point, together with a commitment to try and improve that position.
2 It is recognized that, although the focus of this research was gender relations, these will be cut across and compounded by relations of class and 'race'. However, as others (for example, Dewar 1990) have noted, it is often in terms of gender that an otherwise homogeneous group of PE students might be differently positioned.
3 Evans (1989) has suggested that 'co-education' instead of 'mixed sex' should only be used to refer to those situations where there is a sensitivity to the predispositions children bring to the lesson (abilities, cultural attitudes and expectations, etc.) which often serve to set boys and girls apart. As the discussion in this chapter describes, my use of this term here may be somewhat optimistic.
4 The research is a PhD project based in the School of Education of the Open University.
5 See Siraj-Blatchford (1991) for an account of how racism structures black students' experiences of teacher education.
6 The term 'girlie' was used by some male students to refer to women in ways similar to those terms used by boys in schools to describe girls reported elsewhere (see, for example, Lees 1987). It had two connotations. First, it was used to describe women who were worth 'pursuing' sexually. Literature put out by the Students' Union (the president of which was male) reinforced an ethos within the informal student culture of what Holly (1989) has called a predatory

heterosexuality. 'Girlies' were constantly being described as 'available', to be 'had', and so on. The president, for example, proclaimed in one leaflet that his major aim of office was to 'have' as many girlies as possible. Second, the term was used to describe women PE students' 'inferior' physical abilities compared to the men (comments such as 'She won't be able to do it, she's only a girlie' were common).

7 See Brackenridge (1990) for an exploration of issues of sexual power relations between coaches and athletes.

8 Brittan (1989) uses the term 'masculinism' to describe the ideology which both justifies and naturalizes male domination.

References

Acker, S. (ed.) (1989) *Teachers, Gender and Careers*, Falmer, London.

Amos, V. and Parmar, P. (1987) 'Resistance and responses of the experiences of black girls in Britain' in M. Arnot and G. Weiner (eds), *Gender and the Politics of Schooling*, Hutchinson Education, London, pp. 211–22.

Arnot, M. (1982) 'Male hegemony, social class and women's education', *Journal of Education*, vol. 164, no. 1, pp. 64–89.

Arnot, M. (1984) 'How should we educate our sons?' in R. Deem (ed.), *Coeducation Reconsidered*, Open University Press, Milton Keynes, pp. 37–55.

Askew, S. and Ross, C. (ed.) (1988) *Boys Don't Cry: Boys and Sexism in Education*, Open University Press, Milton Keynes.

Benyon, J. (1989) 'A school for men: an ethnographic case study of routine violence in schooling' in S. Walker and L. Barton (eds), *Politics and the Processes of Schooling*, Open University Press, Milton Keynes, pp. 191–217.

Brackenridge, C. (1990) 'Myth, drama or crisis? Cross-gender coaching relationships', *Coaching Focus*, Summer, pp. 1–6.

Brah, A. and Minhas, R. (1985) 'Structural racism or cultural difference: schooling for Asian girls' in G. Weiner (ed.), *Just a Bunch of Girls*, Open University Press, Milton Keynes, pp. 14–25.

Brittan, A. (1989) *Masculinity and Power*, Basil Blackwell, Oxford.

Burchell, H. and Millman, V. (1989) *Changing Perspectives on Gender: New Initiatives in Secondary Education*, Open University Press, Milton Keynes.

Burgess, R. (1989) 'Something you learn to live with? Gender and Inequality in a comprehensive school', *Gender and Education*, vol. 1, no. 2, pp. 155–64.

Carrington, B. and Leaman, O. (1986) 'Equal opportunities and physical education' in J. Evans (ed.), *Physical Education, Sport Schooling: Studies in the Sociology of Physical Education*, Falmer, Lewes, pp. 215–26.

Connell, R.W. (1987) *Gender and Power*, Polity Press, Cambridge.

Connell, R.W. (1990) 'An iron man: the body and some contradictions of hegemonic masculinity' in M.A. Messner and D.F. Sabo (eds), *Sport, Men and the Gender Order: Critical Feminist Perspectives*, Human Kinetics, Leeds, pp. 83–95.

Cunnison, S. (1989) 'Gender joking in the staffroom' in S. Acker (ed.), *Teachers, Gender and Careers*, Falmer, London, pp. 151–67.

Curry, T.J. (1991) 'Fraternal bonding in the locker room: a profeminist analysis of talk about competition and women', *Sociology of Sport*, 8, pp. 119–35.

Denscombe, M. (1982) 'The hidden pedagogy and its implications for teacher training', *British Journal of Sociology of Education*, vol. 3, no. 3, pp. 249–69.

Dewar, A. (1990) 'Oppression and privilege in physical education: struggles in the negotiation of gender in a university programme' in D. Kirk and R. Tinning (eds), *Physical Education, Curriculum and Culture: Critical Issues in the Contemporary Crisis*, Falmer, Basingstoke, pp. 67–99.

De Lyon, H. and Widdowson Migniuolo, F. (eds) (1989) *Women Teachers: Issues and Experiences*, Open University Press, Milton Keynes.

Dunning, E. (1973) 'The rugby club as a type of "male preserve": some sociological notes', *International Review for the Sociology of Sport*, 8, pp. 3–4.

EOC (1989) *Formal Investigation Report: Initial Teacher Education in England and Wales*, EOC, Manchester.

Evans, J. (1989) 'Swinging from the crossbar: equality and opportunity in the physical education curriculum', *British Journal of Physical Education*, vol. 20, no. 2, pp. 84–7.

Fletcher, S. (1984) *Women First: The Female Tradition in English Physical Education 1880–1980*, Athlone, London.

Flintoff, A. (1991) 'Dance, masculinity and teacher education', *British Journal of Physical Education*, vol. 22, no. 4, pp. 31–5.

Flintoff, A. (forthcoming) 'Gender, physical education and initial teacher education' in J. Evans (ed.), *Equality, Education and Physical Education*, Falmer, Basingstoke.

Griffin, P. (1989) 'Gender as a socialising agent in physical education' in T. Templin and P. Schemp (eds), *Socialisation into Physical Education: Learning to Teach*, Benchmark Press, Indianapolis, pp. 219–32.

Halson, J. (1989) 'The sexual harassment of young women' in L. Holly (ed.), *Girls and Sexuality: Learning and Teaching*, Open University Press, Milton Keynes, pp. 130–42.

Holly, L. (ed.) (1989) *Girls and Sexuality: Learning and Teaching*, Open University Press, Milton Keynes.

Jackson, D. (1990) *Unmasking Masculinity: A Critical Autobiography*, London, Unwin Hyman.

Kelly, L. (1992) 'Not in front of the children: responding to right wing agendas on sexuality and education' in M. Arnot and L. Barton (eds), *Voicing Concerns: Sociological Perspectives on Contemporary Educational Reforms*, Triangle Books, Oxford, pp. 20–40.

Kessler, S., Ashenden, D., Connell, R. and Dowsett, G. (1987) 'Gender relations in secondary schooling' in M. Arnot and G. Weiner (eds), *Gender and the Politics of Schooling*, Hutchinson Education, London, pp. 223–36.

Leaman, O. (1984) *Sit on the Sidelines and Watch the Boys Play: Sex Differentiation in Physical Education*, Longman for Schools Council, York.

Lees, S. (1987) 'The structure of sexual relations in school' in M. Arnot and G. Weiner (eds), *Gender and the Politics of Schooling*, Hutchinson Education, London, pp. 175–86.

Lenskyj, H. (1987) 'Female sexuality and women's sport', *Women's Studies International Forum*, vol. 10, no. 4, pp. 381–6.

Leonard, D. (1989) 'Gender and initial teacher training' in H. De Lyon and F. Widdowson Migniuolo (eds), *Women Teachers: Issues and Experiences*, Open University Press, Milton Keynes, pp. 23–36.

Mahony, P. (1985) *School for the Boys? Coeducation Reassessed*, Hutchinson, London.

Mahony, P. (1989) 'Sexual violence and mixed schools' in C. Jones and P. Mahony (eds), *Learning Our Lines: Sexuality and Social Control*, The Women's Press, London, pp. 157–90.

Mapp, L. (1982) 'Working with boys' in EOC, *Report of Conference on Equal Opportunities: What's in it for Boys?* EOC, Manchester.

McKay, J., Gore, J. and Kirk, D. (1990) 'Beyond the limits of technocratic PE', *Quest*, vol. 42, no. 1, pp. 40–51.

Messner, M. (1987) 'The life of a man's seasons: male identity in the life course of the jock' in M. S. Kimmel (ed.), *Changing Men: New Directions in Research on Men and Masculinity*, Sage, London, pp. 53–67.

Scraton, S. (1985) 'Losing ground: the implications for girls of mixed physical education', paper presented at the British Educational Research Association, Sheffield.

Scraton, S. (1987) 'Gender and physical education: ideologies of the physical and the politics of sexuality' in S. Walker and L. Barton (eds), *Changing Policies, Changing Teachers: New Directions for Schooling?* Open University Press, Milton Keynes, pp. 169–89.

Scraton, S. (1992) *Shaping Up to Womanhood: Gender and Physical Education,* Open University Press, Milton Keynes.

Scraton, S. (forthcoming) 'Equality, co-education and physical education in secondary schooling' in J. Evans (ed.), *Equality, Education and Physical Education,* Falmer, Lewes.

Sikes, P. (1991) 'Nature took its course? Student teachers and gender awareness', *Gender and Education,* vol. 3, no. 2, pp. 145–62.

Siraj-Blatchford, I. (1991) 'A study of black students' perceptions of racism in initial teacher education', *British Educational Research Journal,* vol. 17, no. 1, pp.35–50.

Stanworth, M. (1983) *Gender and Schooling: A Study of Sexual Divisions in the Classroom,* Hutchinson, London.

Walby, S. (1990) *Theorising Patriarchy,* Basil Blackwell, Cambridge.

Whitson, D. (1990) 'Sport in the social construction of masculinity' in M.A. Messner and D.F. Sabo (eds), *Sport, Men and the Gender Order: Critical Feminist Perspectives,* Human Kinetics, Leeds, pp. 19–29.

Whyte, J., Deem, R., Kant, L. and Cruickshank, M. (eds) (1985) *Girl Friendly Schooling,* Methuen, London.

Wood, J. (1984) 'Groping towards sexism: boys' sex talk' in A. McRobbie and M. Nava (eds), *Gender and Generation,* Macmillan, London.

CHAPTER 7

The Heart of the Matter? Student Teachers' Experiences in School

GILL CROZIER and IAN MENTER

Introduction

This chapter deals with some of the experiences of racism and sexism that women and black students endure while on school experience. School experience, in the form of either blocks (often referred to as 'teaching practice') or serial attachments, has always been an essential ingredient of the initial education and training of teachers. But now, as initial teacher *education* moves towards increasingly school-based *training*, it becomes even more important to address the significance of student experience in school. There is a danger that these developments may lead all students, black and white, women and men, to be even less prepared to deal with racism and sexism at both a professional and personal level.

In order to contextualize our discussion about school experience, we begin by presenting certain features of the contemporary debates about teacher education, first through considering the socio-political context and second through considering aspects of the professional context of teacher education. We then present some personal accounts of students' experiences in schools, before suggesting some strategies for future action.

The socio-political context

The recent impact of the new right on educational policy has been well documented (Demaine 1988; Ball 1990). There are, however, two aspects of the pronouncements emanating from the new right and the government that are central to our concerns in this chapter. These are, first, the attack on the 'barmy theory' allegedly promoted by teacher education institutions, and second, the call for initial teacher 'training' to be entirely or largely school-based. For example, Sheila Lawlor (1990), of the Centre for Policy Studies, dismisses educational theory within teacher training [*sic*] courses as a diversion from 'subject' teaching and as a subversion of practical teaching. Lawlor advocates the abolition of Bachelor of Education (BEd) and Postgraduate Certificate of Education (PGCE) courses and the establishment of 'on-the-job' training. The Hillgate Group (1989) (which includes Baroness Cox and Roger Scruton) pours further scorn upon teacher education in its condemnation, for instance, of courses being dominated by 'theory' and 'sociology' which are 'irrelevant' and 'biased'.

Along with other educational changes, we have increasingly seen the adoption by the government of the new right's ideas for teacher education (although perhaps now more appropriately it should be called 'training'), in particular with the emphasis on subject study and the de-emphasis of education studies, and with the introduction of the largely school-based articled teachers scheme (see Hextall *et al.* 1991). More recently we have seen an acceleration of moves towards more school-based training.

Having said this, however, teacher education institutions have been, for some time, developing greater involvement with schools in a variety of ways and have placed much emphasis upon breaking down 'the theory/practice divide' which did characterize many courses (Alexander 1984). Some institutions, for example, now require their students on a four-year BEd to spend the equivalent of a year in school (HMI 1991). Some institutions have adopted a system of teacher tutors where the teacher in school is responsible for supervising and assessing the student with minimal involvement of the institution-based tutor.

In principle, the development of partnerships between schools and HEIs and the enhancement of the relationship between theory and practice can be very productive. However, the most recent changes, with their emphasis on training schools and a lessening of the role of the HEI, are based on a very different conception of teaching to that which is currently held within the profession and represent the continuing erosion of an intellectual basis for students' preparation as teachers.

The reasons for our disagreements are manifold, but we confine our remarks here to the central issues of this chapter. What, then, is the significance of these changes with respect to 'race' and gender issues? The juxtaposition of the attack on educational theory and the advocation of school-based training is not presented here as a conspiracy against the anti-racist and anti-sexist lobbies. However, in making their criticism of educational theory, the new right do frequently make critical reference to gender issues and to multi-cultural/anti-racist education (see, for example, Honeyford 1983; Flew 1984; Pearce 1985). These criticisms have been carried through into the attacks on teacher education, cited above. One such writer, Dennis O'Keeffe (1990) even refers to 'equality pimps' in teacher education establishments – see Menter (1992) for a review of these statements with regard to 'race'. Moreover, the 1992 draft criteria for the accreditation of teacher training courses, with their emphasis on skills and competences, reinforce the view that prospective teachers should not be concerned about the wider issues of society. As Barton *et al.* (1992) have argued, if teachers lack an understanding of structural inequalities they are unlikely to be able to meet the needs of many of the children whom they will come to teach. On the other hand, if teachers were to develop such critical insights they might transfer them to their pupils, but of course such critical reflection is not one of the government's aims for education in the 1990s.

In eschewing educational theory and by lessening the time spent in the HEI, the possibilities for promoting an understanding of 'race' and gender issues and for developing an anti-racist and anti-sexist ideology as part of that, is likely to be diminished. It would then rest entirely on the commitment of individual teachers and schools. In addition to impeding the opportunities for students to develop these understandings, the support available for women and black students in dealing with sexism and/or racism at a personal level is also likely to be reduced.

The professional context

In the previous section we have implied that HEIs are successful at promoting anti-racist and anti-sexist approaches within their teacher education courses. We turn now to consider the extent to which this is actually the case.

'Permeation' has become the dominant term to describe the mode through which issues of 'equality in education' are addressed in these courses. While there is considerable variation in the detail of practice (see, for example, Crozier *et al.* 1988), some consistency has been brought about as a result of the implementation of the criteria for accreditation of teacher education courses which were published in 1989. In order for the Council for the Accreditation of Teacher Education (CATE) to recommend to the Secretary of State that a course be accredited, the institution has had to demonstrate that students will learn to 'guard against preconceptions based on the race, gender, religion or other attributes of pupils and understand the need to promote equal opportunities' (DES 1989).

There must be concern that the draft criteria included in the January 1992 Consultation Document on *The Reform of Initial Teacher Training* (DES 1992) make no mention whatever of equal opportunities matters. Notwithstanding the point made earlier, while these new criteria focus on outcomes and competences rather than on 'content', there is no reason why skills or competences should not be related to equal opportunities.

Nevertheless, it is far from clear that the existing arrangements have led to effective treatment of 'race' and gender issues on courses. There has been little evidence of permeation being effective as a strategy against racism and sexism within these institutions (ARTEN 1988). There is nothing to prevent the way in which courses meet the 'CATE criterion' mentioned above from being superficial or to guarantee that it is more than an 'academic' exercise. For student teacher behaviour to be changed some active learning is required. Even where very explicit treatment is given to such matters it is very difficult to detect any significant shift in students' behaviour (Menter 1987).

What has been most striking though, in observing these affairs over recent years, is how often there is a very direct contradiction between the espousal of liberal anti-sexist and anti-racist positions by college staff and the lived experience of students and staff. While we consider some of that experience in the next section, it is important to register here the gap between rhetoric and reality which so often exists. This perhaps shows up most clearly of all in the context which is the specific concern of this chapter – that of school experience or teaching practice. While there has been much attention in the recent past on the relationship between schools and HEIs in the teacher training process (see, for example, Booth *et al.* 1990), there has been very little discussion of the application of permeation of equality issues in this context. This is in spite of the fact that many HEIs, LEAs and schools have developed policy statements on 'race' and gender 'equality' during the last decade. There is evidence to suggest that sometimes the uneven development of such policies has led to serious tension between schools and HEIs (Menter 1989).

The balance of power between these 'partners' – the school, the HEI institution and, in some areas, the LEA – is a key contemporary issue in initial teacher education. While much of the discourse in documents from official bodies such as the CNAA, HMI and CATE has been couched in terms of 'equality' in the partnership, this is rarely defined and there is still considerable confusion about respective roles. As we have argued elsewhere (Crozier *et al.* 1990), there has been a degree of ideological closure around the notion of partnership which makes it very difficult to engage in the debate in a critical way without appearing to be reactionary and simply defending 'our' interests as teacher educators. The Secretary of State's intervention in this debate in January 1992 has sharpened its focus considerably. While his proposals at the time of writing only relate to secondary PGCE courses, it is anticipated that other courses will also get 'the treatment' in due course. There is confusion in the proposals between schools 'taking the lead' and the notion of 'a more equal partnership'.

However, if there is something of a contest between schools and higher education at an institutional level, there can also be considerable tension between individuals at an interpersonal level. Within the arrangements which have prevailed hitherto it is all too clear that inequalities of power exist. The notion of the teaching practice 'triad' has been used in much research in this field as a way of understanding the influences on a student during her practice. It is an important notion because it draws attention to the significance of the interrelationships of the three adult participants – student, teacher and tutor. What it has rarely been used for, however, is to explore the power base of those relationships.

The teaching practice triad is unequally balanced in terms of power. It is quite clear that the student is in the weakest position. It is she who is 'inexperienced', who is learning and who is being assessed by the end of the teaching practice, however much this is hedged around by the other two members. Experience and research suggest that for the student both the teacher and the tutor have enormous power. On a day-to-day basis the teacher is likely to be the strongest influence on her and it is usual for students to be very concerned about their relationship with the teacher. However, when it comes to the question of assessment the college-based tutor often plays a more important role than the teacher.

The balance of power between the tutor and the teacher as perceived by themselves would appear to vary considerably according to particular situations. Some tutors feel very intimidated by some teachers and vice versa. From an objective point of view, we might allocate each of them a similar degree of power within the triad. So, to summarize, there are two relatively strong members and one relatively weak member in the normal teaching practice triad.

Now all this has been said without mentioning gender or 'race'. Within a patriarchal society it would be reasonable to assume that power imbalances will be exacerbated where a strong position is occupied by a man. In addition, what may be more or less equal relationships may become unequal when sexes are different. Such imbalances are likely to be manifested in a number of ways but may well include the domination of mixed-sex discussions by male participants (Spender 1980).

In a similar field of study, that of the 'clinical supervision' of practising teachers in the USA, St Maurice (1987) has exposed the unequal distribution of power inherent in the relationship between the teacher and her supervisor. The practice is dressed up in humanistic language by its protagonists (see, for example, Goldhammer *et al.* 1980) and put forward as a democratic and liberal way of achieving professional development, as indicated by Stones (1984, p. 34) in his description of the approach: 'The teacher/supervisor relationship is seen as one of mutuality within a framework of respect for individual autonomy and self-regulated enquiry, analysis, examination and evaluation.' In his critical discussion of clinical supervision St Maurice argues that the underlying reality (which he says most teachers involved are actually well aware of) is one of teachers being assessed and controlled by their managers. The majority of teachers are women, the majority of supervisors are men.

> The writings on clinical supervision are silent about the imbalance of power along gender lines in American schools. The regimes of social and economic power in American education have practically dictated a predominantly female teacher population subordinated to a male managerial elite. (St Maurice 1984, p. 248)

The same silence exists over the gender imbalance in teaching practice supervision in Britain.

With regard to 'race', even less research has been carried out, although, as we shall see shortly, the experience of black students indicates a very similar scenario.

But before turning to this experience, it should also be noted that, even on courses where there is a strong expression of commitment to equality issues, there is evidence that this very rarely leads to effective treatment of these concerns within the teaching practice triad. Research carried out at two institutions (Menter 1989) indicated a 'stasis' within these relationships. This affected both the interpersonal aspects of the triad (for example, male teachers were sometimes very sexist in their behaviour towards female students) and the professional discussions between the triad members (for example, tutors were very loath to raise questions about adopting a more 'multi-cultural' approach to the curriculum). Potentially contentious issues, especially if they might challenge the professionalism of the teacher, were invariably avoided.

Student experience in school

In the context of relative powerlessness which all student teachers experience on teaching practice, it is perhaps not surprising that for black (and particularly black women) students, this can be a time of extreme difficulty. In her study of black students' experiences of teacher education courses,

Siraj-Blatchford (1990, p. 17) came to the conclusion that 'school practice provided the worst experiences of racial discrimination for many black students'. Some quotations from the students in her survey indicate the quality of this experience.

> In an urban, mainly white school the older children, upper infants and Juniors made racist comments such as 'Blacky' and 'Nigger'.

> I did a T.P. in an urban multiracial school. I was placed in a class which is considered by both my tutors and teaching staff to be the worst they have ever seen. I was verbally and physically abused by the children. The only reason why I was placed there is because I am black. They removed a white student yet, despite my pleas to leave, they would not let me. I am ignored by all of the staff. My class teacher treats me as if I am invisible, mainly because I disagree with the way the children are treated, i.e. constant suspensions rather than logical reasoning and a consistent approach.

> I experienced the attitude expressed by teachers and heads in several schools that black students will get jobs because of their colour rather than their ability – indeed better qualified whites would lose out! (Siraj-Blatchford 1990, pp. 17–18)

In a telling narrative by a black student undertaking a BEd degree (Clay *et al.* 1991, p. 27), 'Anita' recounts many of her experiences as the one black student among 150 in her year. She describes her first-year teaching practice:

> I was introduced to my class by the words 'This is Miss R . . . Yes, she is different, isn't she?' I was then asked to talk to the children about India, the place that I was born!! The anger I felt was incredible, and I resorted to embarrassing the teacher by denying that I was born in India (which in fact I was not, I was born in East Africa) but said I was born in Wiltshire, and if she wished I would talk about this! Teaching practices were always times which produced examples of both direct and hidden racism. In my third year practice, my advisor asked my colleagues 'Does she fit in in the staffroom?'. Again, when I complained to senior figures within the institution, I was ignored.
> . . . My final teaching practice summed up the entire experience for me. I was placed in a school where both the class teacher and the headteacher were openly hostile, and in school with me was a student who had previously made quite blatant racist comments. In the first two weeks of the practice, the Head told me that I would only get a 'pass' grading, with the clear

implication that I was 'too confident for his liking'. This was despite the fact that the assessed period of the placement did not even start until the fourth week. Even after this hostile beginning, my advisor expressed satisfaction with my performance, and indicated that I was capable of an outstanding grade. However, the pressure built up through my practice, the racist comments made by the class teacher and parents. On one occasion I overheard one parent say to another in a contemptuous way, 'Well, at least she hasn't got an accent.' . . . When I spoke to my advisor about the way I was being treated, I was made to feel again that I was the problem, that I was using racism as an excuse, and that unless I 'carried on', I would be heavily penalised for 'not achieving professional relationships'. I was told that I had to 'prove' that the school were being racist which, unless the teacher was prepared to admit it to the advisor, could not be done . . .

In the end, I was told by my advisor to 'trust the institution' to take account of the fact that the school's report was biased and would take no account of my ability. I had no choice but to agree. The result was only a low 'Pass' grading, one that I knew was not a true reflection of my performance; I felt that my advisor had simply 'fallen into line'.

This particular student, not surprisingly, was left 'totally disillusioned' by her experience.

These accounts are none the less valid for being anecdotal. Certainly more systematic research is urgently required to investigate the nature of black students' experience in teacher education. In particular, there is a need to look at the pass rates and grades of black students in comparison to those of white. There must be real concern at the apparently high proportion of black students whose 'cases' come up as problems at exam boards often (but not only) relating to teaching practice.

What these accounts clearly illustrate is the feeling of disempowerment which can be experienced by black student teachers when they are in school. Often their HEI has recruited them on the basis of the twin commitments of increasing the number of black teachers and producing a teaching workforce which is committed to equal opportunities. Their actual experience as black people is then either denied or treated tokenistically. Bilingualism, for example, is (incredibly) often seen in a limiting way rather than as indicating a general linguistic aptitude. So one black student, applying for posts at the end of her course and finding she was not being shortlisted, discovered that her college reference indicated that because she spoke English as a second language she was 'best suited to working in an inner-city environment with immigrant children'.

Where black perspectives are more prevalent, for example at the University of North London, which has a significant proportion of black students and relatively high numbers of black teaching staff, the experience can be more positive, as indicated in accounts from students who have entered the BEd from an access course (East and Pitt 1989). One student, referring to her experience on teaching practice, talks of the relationships which developed between her and the black children in the school:

> They confide in me all over the place and I think this intimacy they just give to you, because of what you are. It is absolutely vital to have black teachers as figures of authority around the place and for pupils to see that a lot of issues to do with black kids need first-hand experience. (East and Pitt 1989, p. 44)

However, even here, the teaching practice experience can be negative:

> I was in the staffroom and the school keeper came in and automatically assumed I was a stranger or a cleaner. The fact that I was black, he thought that I couldn't possibly be one of the teachers. It's something that happens quite a lot in this society. You get used to it. I was angry, but no more so than being in other situations – in a restaurant and people thinking I'm serving or cleaning up. (p. 43)

These quotations remind us that these experiences can often be treated merely as 'incidents'. The danger in this is that the structural origins of these manifestations of racism are ignored. While no teacher education establishment which we are aware of has really started to work out how to respond in a coherent and systematic way to racism or sexism within its courses, we are aware of one example from the field of social work education which does provide some significant insights. Drawing partly on accounts by Winston Trew, a black social work tutor, lecturers at South Bank Polytechnic (Trew *et al.* 1990) now South Bank University – have developed a sophisticated analysis of issues of 'race' and student placement within social work education.

They discuss the way in which the 'personal' and the 'professional' aspects of placements become embroiled when there is racial difference within the placement. There are difficult political judgements for black tutors or students to make in these situations:

> anti-racism as a strategy for black students must assume a different existential and socio-ideological premise and starting point. Existential in that it recognises that for black women and men as students racism as a social force is always personally and socially immanent. Socio-ideological in that it must make explicit that racism is essentially a power relation, and that black students forge oppositional strategies either aimed at survival or at direct confrontation in relation to the things at stake for them. These are not so much individual choices but choices predicated by social structure which presents a limited number of options for black students. (Trew *et al.* 1990, p. 39)

These same points could surely be made about the school experience of student teachers.

Strategies for change

The negative experiences for women and black students while on school experience do not arise, it is argued, because schools are more racist establishments than HEIs but rather, because students are potentially more exposed to a wider range of attitudes and ideologies while in school, at the same time as being in a relatively vulnerable position, as outlined above.

With the implementation of the National Curriculum and the demise of local education authority (LEA) power including the influence of their policies on equal opportunities, gender issues and multi-cultural/anti-racist education are being further pushed off the educational agenda. It is likely not only that will students be less prepared to deal with racist and sexist situations but also that the support systems in schools, such as LEA racial and sexual harassment procedures, will be undermined.

In order to arrest this situation and develop support for women and black students in particular, while on school experience, it is necessary to seek both political and professional alliances. At a time when many anti-racist organizations have dissipated, the task of forging appropriate political links looks daunting. However, one starting point may be through the students' union and the teacher unions. Also, many HEIs now have equal opportunities committees which could be drawn on to support the setting-up and maintenance of women's and black students' groups. In addition to this, many former 'public sector' institutions, after having their formal links with LEAs severed, have devised their own policies on sexual and racial harassment or on equal opportunities. In some cases it may be that these are not widely known about among the student body (or even staff) and there may, therefore, be a need for the promotion of such information and for procedures to be developed to cover incidents on school placements.

With regard to the institutions, ongoing staff development for ITE tutors is essential. In our experience 'race' and gender appear infrequently as topics for consideration. However, in addition to discussing ideas and developing understanding, tutors also need to develop strategies for dealing with racism and sexism and need support in implementing these strategies. Paired visiting by tutors when visiting students on school experience may be one useful mechanism for developing skill and confidence in this area.

However, given the current trends in teacher education policy, the crux of school experience must lie in effective partnership with schools. As Her Majesty's Inspectors argued in their report on school-based training (HMI 1991, p. 19), 'the overall quality of training is not a direct product of the amount of time spent in schools or of a particular pattern of school experience but rather of the quality of the teachers and of the relationships between schools and training institutions'.

Although it is as yet unclear what procedures will be adopted with the changes towards more of a school-based model of teacher education, as part of the partnership, we suggest that a contract should be drawn up between HEIs and schools, outlining clearly the commitments, responsibilities and expectations of higher education staff, school staff and students. In many, if not most cases, this is already done informally. However, a more formal approach, which includes a mutual commitment to dealing with racism and sexism at both an institutional and a personal level, is necessary. This is particularly important in order to encourage white male students to take a stance against racist/sexist behaviour. Such an approach is advocated by the Social Work team at South Bank University referred to above (Trew *et al.* 1990). They also call for a more discerning approach to the identification of placements. While in teacher education there are often insufficient places, so making it difficult to apply selection criteria, this should also be an aim to which there is a commitment. The very adoption of a formal contract may well facilitate this.

As part of the developing partnership, even where the teacher takes major responsibility for supervising and assessing the student, we urge the promotion of critical discussions within school experience 'triads', that is between teacher, student and institution-based tutor. We believe that in addition to this there is a need for monitoring and evaluating student supervision. Moreover, with the introduction of mentors – 'designated teachers to undertake the training of students in schools' (Wilkin 1992, p. 18) – mentor training will be a key area of development. Consideration of 'race' and gender issues must become an essential element of mentor training.

Conclusion

It has been argued that students on school experience are likely to be in a more vulnerable position to deal with racism and sexism, in terms of their pedagogy and/or in terms of their personal experiences. With the increase in school-based work and the corresponding demise in Education Studies, students are likely to be even less well prepared than at present.

The central feature of school-based training is the partnership between higher education and schools. It has been argued that the partnership must be based upon a clear commitment to challenging racism and sexism and developing strategies for working in a mutually supportive way towards this end. This would not only benefit the students but also have the potential effect of raising the awareness of serving teachers and thereby improve the quality of education for children.

References

Alexander, R. (1984) 'Innovations and continuity in the initial teacher education curriculum' in R. Alexander, M. Craft and J. Lynch (eds), *Change in Teacher Education*, Holt, Rinehart and Winston, London.

ARTEN (1988) *Permeation: The Road to Nowhere*, Jordanhill College, Glasgow.

Ball, S. (1990) *Politics and Policy Making in Education*, Routledge, London.

Barton, L., Pollard, A. and Whitty, G. (1992) 'Experiencing CATE: the impact of accreditation upon initial training institutions in England', *Journal of Education for Teaching*, vol. 18, pp. 41–57.

Booth, M., Furlong, J. and Wilkin, M. (eds) (1990) *Partnership in Initial Teacher Training*, Cassell, London.

Clay, J., Gadhia, S. and Wilkins, M. (1991) 'Racism and institutional inertia: a 3-D perspective of initial teacher education (disillusionment, disaffection and despair)', *Multicultural Teaching*, vol. 9, no. 3, pp. 26–31.

Crozier, G., Lee, J. and Menter, I. (1988) 'A survey of anti-racist teacher education practice' in ARTEN, *Permeation: The Road to Nowhere*, Jordanhill College, Glasgow.

Crozier, G., Menter, I. and Pollard, A. (1990) 'Changing partnership' in M. Booth, J. Furlong and M. Wilkin (eds), *Partnership in Initial Teacher Training*, Cassell, London.

Demaine, J. (1988) 'Teachers' work, curriculum and the New Right', *British Journal of Sociology of Education*, vol. 9, no. 3, pp. 247–64.

DES (Department of Education and Science) (1989) *Initial Teacher Training: Approval of Courses*. Circular 24/89, DES, London.

DES (1992) *The Reform of Initial Teacher Training, A Consultation Document*, DES, London.

East, P. and Pitt, R. (1989) 'Access to teaching for black women' in H. De Lyon and F. Widdowson Migniuolo (eds), *Women Teachers: Issues and Experiences*, Open University Press, Milton Keynes.

Flew, A. (1984) *Education, Race and Revolution*, Centre for Policy Studies, London.

Goldhammer, R., Anderson, R. and Krazewski, R. (1980) *Clinical Supervision: Special Methods for the Supervision of Teachers*, Holt, Rinehart and Winston, New York.

Hextall, I., Lawn, M., Menter, I., Sidgwick, S. and Walker, S. (1991) *Imaginative Projects, Arguments for a New Teacher Education*, Goldsmiths' College, London.

Hillgate Group (1989) *Learning to Teach*, Claridge Press, London.

HMI (1991) *School-based Initial Teacher Training in England and Wales*, DES, London.

Honeyford, R. (1983) 'Multi-ethnic intolerance', *The Salisbury Review*, vol. 4, Summer, pp. 12–13.

Lawlor, S. (1990) *Teachers Mistaught*, Centre for Policy Studies, London.

Menter, I. (1987) 'Evaluating teacher education: some notes on an anti-racist programme for BEd students', *Multicultural Teaching*, vol. 5, no. 3, pp. 39–42.

Menter, I. (1989) 'Teaching practice stasis: racism, sexism and school experience in initial teacher education', *British Journal of Sociology of Education*, vol. 10, no. 4, pp. 459–73.

Menter, I. (1992) 'The New Right, racism and teacher education: some recent developments', *Multicultural Teaching*, vol. 10, no. 2, pp. 6–9.

O'Keeffe, D. (1990) *The Wayward Elite*, Adam Smith Institute, London.

Pearce, S. (1985) *Education and the Multi-Racial Society*, Monday Club, London.

St Maurice, H. (1987) 'Clinical supervision and power: regimes of instructional management' in T. Popkewitz (ed.), *Critical Studies in Teacher Education*, Falmer, London.

Siraj-Blatchford, I. (1990) 'Positive discrimination: the under-achievement of initial teacher education', *Multicultural Teaching*, vol. 8, no. 2, pp. 14–19.

Spender, D. (1980) *Man Made Language*, Routledge and Kegan Paul, London.

Stones, E. (1984) *Supervision in Teacher Education*, Methuen, London.

Trew, W., Weigars, C. and Weinstein, J. (1990) *Anti-racist Strategies and Student Placements: A College Perspective*, South Bank Polytechnic, London.

Wilkin, M. (ed.) (1992) *Mentoring in Schools*, Kogan Page, London.

Policies, Strategies and Change

Admissions and Outcome: Guidance on How to Improve the Quality of the Student Intake

LYNDA CARR

In 1986 the Equal Opportunities Commission (EOC) and the Commission for Racial Equality (CRE) were presented with the first evidence of prima-facie discrimination on the grounds of sex and 'race' in admissions to higher education. The institution concerned had a high proportion of black students and a reputation for its liberal ethos, but it sifted applications by using a computer program in which women and black applicants were systematically and blatantly penalized. The computer program assessed academic and personal factors which included race and gender. Both 'non-Caucasian' and 'female' factors carried negative weightings and resulted in potential students being rejected for interview solely on the grounds that they were black and/or female.

The findings of the investigation which was conducted by the CRE (1987) make fascinating reading. However, the most important aspect of the matter is that the computer program was designed specifically by an admissions tutor to replace the system of personal sifting which had previously taken place, and to give the same outcomes. Its aim was to remove any inconsistencies in the first stage of the admissions process, and in so doing account was taken of all the criteria which were used in the selection of students. The program replicated exactly the judgements, and correlated perfectly with the personal selections, made by the admissions tutors. Moreover, the bias against women and black applicants was obvious to anyone who saw the program; inequality was so much the norm that no one noticed until one particular tutor took a personal interest in racial and sexual discrimination.

In ITE the process of selecting students who will become effective and successful teachers is fraught with discriminatory pitfalls. The paucity in numbers of black student teachers is a cause for concern, as is the continued sex-stereotyping of subjects in the curriculum. Few admissions tutors are trained either in equal opportunities issues or selection techniques. Guidelines for the admissions process are rare, and criteria exist mainly at the back of someone's mind – although we all somehow know what we are looking for when we see it. Department of Education and Science (DES) policy pays only the faintest lip-service to issues of gender and 'race' in teacher education and it is going to be even harder work to promote gender and 'race' issues where, under new DES policies, teachers are trained other than in the teacher education institutions.

In order to make any assessment of the admissions process relevant, it has to be compared with its outcomes. The ultimate effectiveness of the potential student as a classroom teacher is what selection for a teacher education course is primarily about, and it is with a view to attracting, identifying and training the best potential teachers that gender and 'race' issues are significant in the admissions process. Tutors lament the absence of black and male lower-primary students, but few institutions are setting out actively to increase their numbers. Nor are teacher educators in general taking the necessary initiatives to attract into the teaching profession a much broader cross-section of applicants with a view to improving the outcome and the effectiveness of the training process.

Teacher educators have a responsibility not only to their students, the local authority, and the institutions in which and with which they work, but also to the education service as a whole. After all, the process of admitting students to teacher education is the point at which the quality of the teaching resource is determined, but more particularly it is the point at which good quality education provision begins. The quality of educational provision cannot be improved unless issues of 'race' and gender are given careful consideration in terms of access, process and outcome, and this is as true of admissions to teacher education as it is to the teaching of physics or, indeed, the curriculum of 5–16-year-olds. Weaknesses in the system impact most severely upon women, and black and ethnic minority people, largely because education policy is most often formulated by white men on the basis of their own experience and with other white men in mind. However, the strengthening of the system, and the resolution of problems which an equal opportunities perspective identifies, work in the best interests of everyone and improve systems and standards generally.

A good admissions procedure is one which is consistent, objective, and fair in its application, but which also sets out to attract applicants who have a positive approach to 'race' and gender issues along with their commitment to teaching as a future career. The underlying principle on which such an admissions/outcomes policy is based, is that sexism and racism deny opportunities to learn, and prevent the achievement of educational objectives.

At the moment the outcome of admissions procedures generally is a teaching force which is sex-stereotyped to a degree which is unhelpful to the education process. Young women are still not taking up maths and science-based courses or training and employment, despite their proven ability in these subjects and the economic demand for workers with such skills and qualifications. Young men still do not regard the study of modern European languages as appropriate, despite the widening opportunities for work in the European Community. Sex-stereotyping, which is unjustified and anti-educational, is cutting off thousands of young people from valuable educational experiences, but until they see women and men teachers working together in all subject areas, producing teaching materials which are of interest and relevance to both sexes, heading departments and taking policy decisions, they will not be convinced. And this experience is exacerbated for young black and ethnic minority women and men who have even fewer positive role models and of whom expectations generally are unjustifiably low.

There is a wealth of potential talent outside ITE to which the teaching institutions should be reaching out in their own interests and in the interests of the education service as a whole. Schools want and need teachers who provide *good* role models for all their pupils, who have a wide range of academic and personal experiences, and who reflect and are sensitive to the needs and aspirations of a similarly wide range of pupils. The excuse that such a range of potential teachers does not present itself for admission at the doors of the teacher education institutions is not acceptable – teacher educators should be setting out actively to look for them.

'Equality-proofing' the admissions process

When the EOC investigated ITE institutions in 1989 it reported 'a benign apathy' generally towards equal opportunities issues (EOC 1989). Just about everyone thought equality of opportunity was a good idea but only a few were committed to implementing the necessary changes. Interestingly, many of the initiatives on gender which were taking place at that time had been instigated by students, and it was evident that the institutions were, in many cases, failing to meet the changing expectations of young people.

Recently teacher educators have been challenged by legislative and financial changes which are resulting in added pressure and stress. In such circumstances it is tempting to shelve equal opportunities matters or to put them at the bottom of the agenda. But equal opportunities is essentially about improving policies, practices and outcomes for specific groups in particular but to the benefit of everyone eventually. If issues of gender and 'race' cease to be matters of concern then standards will fall, policies will fail, outcomes will be poor and objectives will fail to be met. The admissions process can be made more effective in terms of attracting and selecting women and men from a wide range of social and ethnic backgrounds (and among those who are disabled), but in order to do this the process itself will need to be improved and the approach to admissions become more professional and better managed.

There can be little doubt that many teacher educators do recognize the need to break down 'race' and gender stereotyping in the initial education of teachers. The need is for collective action locally, regionally and nationally. Black and ethnic minority applicants for teaching courses, like many mature applicants and the minority of women and men who are breaking new ground in traditionally stereotyped subject areas, often enter teacher training by circuitous and haphazard routes.

Systematic and widely-targeted recruitment strategies are needed in order to encourage more good-quality applicants from previously underrepresented sources.

Advertising

Advertising of courses locally and nationally, through new and innovative mechanisms as well as the traditional vehicles, is to be encouraged. Some potential students who are black are likely to read newspapers and listen to programmes from the ethnic minority media, and often in their own indigenous languages. Mature students require a different approach from school-leavers and postgraduates. Institutions which always advertise in the same place, using (largely) the same material, will attract the same type of applicant over and over again. Similarly, word-of-mouth recruitment and personal recommendations, flattering though they may be, will guarantee more of the same. More of the same may be comforting to some tutors who resist the challenges which issues of gender and 'race' throw up, but a training course which is based on comfortable mediocrity will not produce an outcome of quality.

The final form of advertising material needs careful checking for sexist, racist (and ageist) inferences. A text which is perfect in all respects can be destroyed by its accompanying visual images: photographs should include female, male, black and disabled students and staff, and cartoons/line drawings should be checked very carefully. It is all too easy to offend and deter potentially excellent teachers by crude drawing, and attempts at humour do not always travel well.

Despite the Interpretation Act of 1978, it is not acceptable to use the male pronoun throughout to advertising material, with a small disclaimer to the effect that this is intended to include women as well. Women do not, on the whole, accept this as equal treatment and are likely to choose a course which recognizes their existence by referring to them in their own right.

Selection

Selection procedures vary greatly according to whether courses are over- or undersubscribed. Even in cases where admissions tutors are faced with reducing hundreds of applications to a relatively small number, all applicants who meet the minimum criteria should be interviewed. If this is absolutely impossible, then the criteria for a first sift should be agreed formally by all tutors concerned, undertaken by at least two people, and controlled by a senior member of staff. Criteria should be checked for factors which discriminate directly by treating applicants less favourably on the grounds of sex, 'race' or disability, and also those which discriminate indirectly because certain groups are unable to comply with them even though the criteria apply to everyone. In addition, all black and all disabled applicants, whether they meet the criteria or not, should be interviewed or offered an advisory interview. Both the applicant and the interviewer are likely to learn a lot, and either a reapplication or a referral to another course may give a positive outcome of value to everyone concerned.

Undersubscribed courses bring problems of their own, particularly where failure to meet student targets results in reduced funding. Undersubscription does, however, focus the mind on creative new ways to recruit students from previously untapped sources, and offers opportunities to promote equality of opportunity initiatives in the recruitment process.

The process of filling places on a 'first come, first served' basis benefits early applicants and those lucky few who apply very late and pick up places from which there are often unexplained drop-outs. The 'first-come' system is designed to benefit both the institution and those applicants who are turned down and then apply elsewhere. However, from an equal opportunities point of view it creates problems, mainly because it offers no opportunity to consider the body of potential applicants as a whole. It is possible, for example, to interview and select a course full of white students before a single application form from a black applicant appears.

'First come, first served' is unlikely to constitute indirect discrimination on the ground of sex,[1] but if, for example, there were problems with translating information, and applications from black candidates were received later in general, then allegations of indirect discrimination on the ground of 'race' could be made, and the question of whether the system is justifiable would come under the scrutiny of the courts.

There is no doubt that some surreptitious 'balancing' of male and female applicants goes on, and that candidates who would have been offered a place, but for their sex, are consequently rejected. Such a practice is potentially unlawful.

Monitoring of the 'first come' procedure is advisable in order to ascertain whether or not those applicants who are selected are representative of all applicants. In order to do this, a notional cut-off date would have to be agreed by the institution, and applications before and after the cut-off date compared with the applications in total. The selection of students is an important aspect of an institution's equal opportunities policy, and the selection procedure, together with the equality audit, should be monitored as an integral part of the implementation and development of the policy.

The interview process

The interview process is one of the clearest reflections of the effectiveness of an institution's equal opportunities policy. The content is an internal matter, but the following recommendations are made by the Equal Opportunities Commission and the Commission for Racial Equality.

1 At least two tutors of both sexes (plus a school-based teacher where appropriate) should interview applicants. No tutor should ever interview an applicant alone.
2 One tutor should interview all candidates, so that he or she has an overview of the student intake as a whole.
3 The qualities which are being sought from applicants should be decided beforehand at a meeting of all interviewers and relevant staff. Interviewers should keep a record of the criteria and what is agreed for use throughout the interviewing period.
4 The questions which will be asked, and who will ask them, should also be agreed and recorded, bearing in mind the qualities which candidates are required to demonstrate.
5 If staff from teaching practice schools are involved in the interviewing process, they should also comply with the agreed person specification, selection criteria and arrangements for asking questions. Where interviews take place in schools and involve the observation of potential students and school pupils, consistency of approach is particularly important.
6 Records of all interviews should be kept, indicating why

applicants were accepted or rejected. A simple grading system alongside each question is adequate. Records should be kept for six months.

7 Questions which could be interpreted as discriminatory should be avoided, such as 'What will you do if you get married before the end of your training?' and 'Are you able to tone down your accent, if necessary?'.

8 Questions to mature applicants should be phrased carefully. Clearly they need to know that a full-time commitment is required in order to complete the course successfully, but at the same time it is not acceptable to assume that mature women have domestic responsibilities whereas mature men do not. Questions which are based upon stereotyped assumptions about women's and men's roles or about racial stereotypes should not be asked.

Two general points are particularly important. First, the same leading questions should be asked of every applicant so that everyone is given the opportunity to demonstrate whether or not they have the qualities which are being sought. Follow-up questions will inevitably vary but the basic structure of every interview should be the same, with a core of comparable information emerging from each. Second, interviewers should be trained in interviewing techniques by the institution's equal opportunities officer, or by an external equal opportunities trainer.

Every applicant should be measured against explicit criteria which have been agreed and are understood by every tutor who interviews applicants. The criteria should be clear at all times and must include an understanding of the educational implications of sexist and racist attitudes and a positive commitment to teaching girls and boys from all racial backgrounds. Sexism and racism deny opportunities to learn and are wholly at variance with successful teaching and a high quality of educational provision.

It is important, when planning an admissions interview, not to lose sight of the eventual outcome of the course. Individuals who present themselves for a Postgraduate Certificate of Education (PGCE) have little time in three terms to modify their prejudices, and PGCE tutors are well aware of the importance of selecting students who already demonstrate the personal qualities required in an effective teacher. BEd courses, on the other hand, offer considerably more time in which to develop the qualities they regard as important, and may choose a potential teacher who is interesting to work with in the longer term – in which case the criteria for what constitutes 'interesting' should be defined very clearly.

Admissions interviews should be given time, care and attention; for while it is probably true to say that tutors spend a lot of time thinking and worrying about interviewing, it is also true that the process itself is too often unstructured, over-subjective and, as a result, inconsistent. Few institutions provide guidelines for selecting and interviewing students, and very few train admissions staff other than in how to fill in admissions forms. In the absence of any direction and guidance, individual tutors devise their own criteria for selection, often independently and without putting anything down on paper. Ad-hocery, even when it is informed and well intentioned, runs counter to good equal opportunities practice. In circumstances where black students are underrepresented, and sex-stereotyping in the curriculum is still undermining educational objectives, the process needs to be managed both more professionally and with greater awareness of gender and 'race' issues.

Equality objectives

Teacher educators create and develop a national resource which impacts upon the well-being of the country's social and economic affairs, as well as the personal fufilment of the individual, and this can be an important motivator for action on gender and 'race' issues in admissions procedures. Equality objectives are, therefore, an important management tool for all teacher education institutions, and the setting and evaluating of equality objectives are key processes in ensuring a good outcome from the admissions procedure. Quotas are unlawful in UK equal opportunities legislation,[2] but the profile of the student population in any institution should be expected to reflect broadly the population as a whole. Moreover, the same general approach should apply to individual courses within institutions. The need nationally is for a teaching force of women and men of all ages from a variety of racial groups, teaching in all sectors, and employed at all grades. Such a workforce not only offers the widest range of skills, experience and teaching approaches to pupils, but also provides much needed role models, particularly for female and black pupils which, in turn, raise pupils' expectations and consequently improve performance.

There is no blueprint for an equal opportunities admissions policy and its associated equality objectives, because the circumstances of individual institutions necessitate different approaches and emphases. However, an equality objective always has three integrated stages in its achievement:

1 Basic information is obtained in order to assess the current situation and identify a base for measurable action (an equality audit).
2 Action is identified and undertaken by a designated person, or group of people, within an agreed timescale.
3 The outcome of the action is evaluated.

Additionally, in order to be effective, the objective should be negotiated and agreed with the people involved, and responsibility for implementation and evaluation must rest at a senior level with someone who has the authority to make decisions and implement policy.

The basic question is whether an institution's admissions procedure results in the admission of students who have the potential to become effective and successful teachers in terms of meeting pupils' needs, and with particular reference to issues of gender and 'race'. In fact, if the needs of pupils are considered, then issues of 'race' and gender arise immediately because they are still significant determinants of educational outcome.

Equality audit

An equality audit is where the process of reviewing admissions procedures and setting equality objectives begins. The institution as a whole should know the composition of its student body, and information should be collected, analysed and monitored about students' sex, ethnic origin,[3] age, family status, previous relevant experience, and how they heard about and why they applied for the course. Ideally, all this information should be collected from everyone who applies to the institution, or at least from all those who meet the national criteria for entry to teacher education. Certainly everyone who is interviewed should be asked to provide this information (usually in the form of a questionnaire) so that the institution will know whether or not certain groups are over- or underrepresented, which students are, or are not, being interviewed, and so on.

It is important to emphasize that the audit questionnaires must not be used during the course of the admissions process; they are essentially management information which will shape future policies. It is also important to emphasize that responsibility for an equality audit should lie with administrative and not academic staff, and they should be located centrally and at a senior level.

Once the picture of the institution is clear, in terms of its student population, then the issues arising from the audit can be identified. What, for example, are the implications for the institution, its teaching practice schools, primary education nationally, and the expectations of the under-tens, if its primary and lower-primary courses are comprised solely of white women in their early twenties? Quotas may not be set, but every institution should be formulating management equality objectives in terms of improving its equal opportunities profile and ensuring that the teaching workforce is able to offer to schools and pupils a wide and relevant range of experience and skills.

Every aspect of the admissions process should be scrutinized in order to ensure that gender and 'race'-related issues do not deter potential applicants.

National and local equal opportunity policies

You have to look hard to find even a nod in the direction of a national policy for equal opportunities in higher education, even after almost twenty years of legislation. In 1984 the DES published criteria for the approval of teacher education courses which stated:

> Students should be prepared . . . to teach the full range of pupils with their diversity of ability, behaviour, social background and ethnic origins. They will need to learn how to respond flexibly to such diversity and to guard against preconceptions based on the race or sex of pupils. (DES 1984)

However, the extent to which these criteria have been met has never been assessed or evaluated by the DES in subsequent reports.

The Association for Teacher Education in Europe (1987) found no evidence of any systematic attempt to develop an equal opportunities curriculum for initial teacher training. Despite this, there are examples to be found, throughout Britain, of institutions which are formulating and implementing successful policies, often at departmental level, and almost inevitably as a result of a personal initiative, at least initially. If issues of gender and race were being taken seriously by the policy-makers at national level, equality objectives would be among the criteria for funding and other contractual matters. Departmental objectives would feed into institutional objectives, and national policies would both influence and be informed by evaluation of institutional policies. The Education Reform Act (ERA) 1988 was always in danger of damaging its aims for improved educational quality by placing greater emphasis on a political than an educational justification for its content, and this has proved to be the case as far as issues of gender and 'race' are concerned. Neither of these important educational issues has been addressed by the ERA or by any consequent legislative amendments to it.

An equal opportunities policy, on paper, is to be found in almost every HEI in the UK. However, very few policies are being implemented to the point where attitudes and behaviour are changing in line with the policy. Responsibility for ensuring that equality objectives are met lies everywhere and nowhere; sometimes they are not even known about by the very people who can contribute to their achievement. Direction and expectation, in the form of national policy, are absent. There is an almost wilful reluctance among the national policy-makers to acknowledge the adverse effect of sexism and racism on the teaching and learning process. The shortage of teachers in certain subjects is lamented but the fact that 'shortage subjects' – mathematics, modern languages and technology – are also the most heavily sex-stereotyped subjects is ignored.

Anecdotal evidence is also emerging that pressure to increase and fill places (with the attendant financial penalty for failing to do so) is undermining equal opportunities policies. Admissions tutors freely admit that they accept candidates whom they would not consider as potential teachers if they were not under pressure to meet targets.

None of this is acceptable to those who are striving to educate teachers in ways which will enhance the quality of teaching. Nor is it good news for pupils whose opportunities to learn continue to be limited by prejudice and expediency. Gender and 'race' are very significant determinants of educational outcome in the UK – a clear indication that the objective of fulfilling individual potential is not being met. Unjustifiably different and lower expectations of girls and black and ethnic minority pupils result in a massive waste of skills and resources nationally, and the teaching profession is no exception. It is, perhaps, more culpable though, because as a profession it is faced daily with the causes and effects of its failure to address seriously the issues of gender and 'race'.

A good equal opportunities admissions policy for teacher education institutions is the point at which outcomes like these are changed. The EOC (1989) reported a desire on the part of many institutions to recruit high-calibre students with positive attitudes towards equal opportunities, and found a high correlation between the two. Nevertheless, there is still a strong undercurrent of indifference and resistance to equal opportunities initiatives among teacher educators and academics generally. Equal opportunities in teaching is not about policing discriminatory attitudes and practices, but about actively promoting good professional practice in the interests of greater effectiveness. A more successful outcome of the teacher education process will only be achieved when the implications of 'race' and gender awareness are recognized at the outset, in the admissions process itself.

Notes

1 Indirect sex discrimination occurs when a requirement which is applied equally to both women and men has a statistically relevant disproportionate impact, is unjustifiable, and detrimental (Sex Discrimination Act 1975, Section 1[1][b]).
2 The concept of equality in UK legislation under the Sex Discrimination Act 1975 and the Race Relations Act 1976 is premised on the rights of the individual. Quotas are unlawful and class action is not

included. Selection processes, under UK legislation, must result in the selection of the best person for the job. It is lawful, however, in specific situations of underrepresentation, to encourage under-represented groups to apply.

3 The Commission for Racial Equality recommends the following basic ethnic classification: white; black (Caribbean); black (African); black (other); Indian; Pakistani; Bangladeshi; Chinese; other (CRE Press Statement: *Ethnic Classification System Recommended by CRE*, 7 December 1988).

References

Association for Teacher Education in Europe (1987) *Equal Opportunities for Girls and Boys: a Curriculum Framework for Teacher Education with Guidelines for Action*, Brussels.

CRE (1987) *Report of a Formal Investigation into St. George's Hospital Medical School*, London.

DES (1984) *ITT: Approval of Courses*, Circular 3/84, 13 April.

EOC (1989) *Formal Investigation Report: Initial Teacher Training in England and Wales*, EOC, Manchester.

CHAPTER 9

Moving Beyond Permeation: Courses in Teacher Education

JOHN CLAY and ROSALYN GEORGE

Introduction

In this chapter we argue for 'race' and gender equality to be considered as part of an overall understanding of social justice. We accept that inequalities in practice are multi-dimensional and that their effects manifestly impact one upon the other. We therefore question the desirability of maintaining their separateness, for this polarization only serves to dilute and divide the struggle for social justice. We would claim that the ability to combat racism and sexism is central to the education and professional development of all teachers, and to achieving equality and social justice in education.

We examine the influence of the Council for the Accreditation of Teacher Education (CATE) on the design and delivery of initial teacher education (ITE) courses, and how varying interpretations of imprecise CATE criteria have affected 'race' and gender equality programmes. The absence of any reference to equal opportunities in the current consultative document for the reform of ITE (DES 1992), including the proposal to shift a major part of the responsibility for student teachers on secondary Postgraduate Certificate in Education (PGCE) courses from institutions to schools, has serious implications and requires a considered response. The modularization of ITE courses (BA and BEd) could further erode the study of equality issues, and this threat is highlighted. Finally, we explore the possibilities for the development of an anti-oppression curriculum.

'Race', gender and reformism

We consider equality as a concept going beyond the liberal model of equality of opportunity which attempts to provide a basic legal framework, seemingly giving everyone, regardless of class, gender, ethnicity, religion, sexuality or disability, an equal chance to compete. This model fails in practice because it does not take into account the different starting points of individuals and groups and ignores the processes subsequently employed in the practice of equal opportunities. The Race Relations Act (1976) and the Sex Discrimination Act (1975) do appear to be quite radical at the macro-political level but are of little benefit to thousands of our citizens who face personal and institutional discrimination in their daily lives. Equality of access to law, or equality of treatment before the law, is itself part of the structure that maintains and reinforces inequalities.

Attempts have been made by organized movements in education such as the National Association of Multiracial Education (NAME), which subsequently became the National Antiracist Movement in Education, and the Multicultural/Antiracist Education (MCARE) programme in the Strathclyde Region of Scotland, to achieve a more radical form of equality of opportunity than that which was evident up to the 1980s, but these were still clearly rooted to the liberal model of equality. These reformist movements have campaigned to change the conditions of competition in capitalism by the legislative management of social conditions (Clay and Cole 1991). They were concerned with promoting positive images of the discriminated and the disadvantaged, and to this end ushered in a plethora of curriculum initiatives in education that could for the sake of brevity be described as the 'girl-friendly' and multi-culturalist approaches with respect to gender and 'race' inequalities. These initiatives focused on influencing individual ethics and morality and settled for the soft option of the cultural/psychological view of racism and sexism. They reinforced perceptions that individuals and communities were 'the problem' and, in doing so, placed the onus for change on those who already carried the burden of discrimination, while exonerating those in power and society at large from direct and indirect responsibility.

'Girl-friendly' and multi-cultural curriculum initiatives were clearly recognized as inadequate by those in education who had to deal with the deep-seated racism and sexism on a daily basis. The failure of the reformist tendencies to address the underlying issues led to demands from organized groups of women, black and other ethnic minority groups for the development of a political discourse that was informed by anti-racist and anti-sexist analyses and strategies. This pressure from the grass roots was instrumental in shaping the 'equal opportunities' policies that were developed by the Inner London Education Authority (ILEA). ILEA's *Policy for Equality* (1985) went beyond the liberal concept of equal access and viewed education as a means of challenging the status quo. This potential for organized resistance to the hegemonic power structures was clearly recognized by the establishment, and, as a result, ILEA was finally abolished by the Thatcher government. However, it would be misleading to convey an impression that genuine advances in policy were uniformly translated into effective practice throughout its area of jurisdiction. We must remember that ILEA seemed incapable of meeting the desperate educational needs of the Bangladeshi community in Tower Hamlets, where many school-age children were denied the right to a basic education. Nevertheless, the democratic left, as represented by ILEA, was critical in the evolution of a politics for equality in which education was acknowledged as a crucial component in the struggle. Equality, defined in discrete terms of 'race', class, gender and other oppressions, influenced the development of policies and practices concerned with equality in many schools and also in a few ITE institutions.

CATE criteria and influence on course design – past, present and future

The criteria for approval of teacher education courses was first instituted in England and Wales and was set out in detail via Circular 3/84 (DES 1984). The criteria laid down for the first time the principles that should underpin the content of teacher education courses for primary and secondary and for undergraduate and postgraduate courses. There was a clear delineation regarding what should be subject study, school experience and practice, and education and professional studies. Teacher education was to be subjected to a curriculum that was controlled from the centre – a National Curriculum, in effect.

Criticisms of the criteria relating to social justice issues were in the main levelled at the tokenistic approach adopted by the circular. Paragraphs 11 and 12 of the document acknowledged the reality of the presence of black and other ethnic minorities within the education system, despite its inability to state that society and thus the education system is structured by class, 'race' and gender, and that schooling underpins and perpetuates the power relations that these dynamic factors embody. The criteria outlined in Circular 3/84 were criticised by radical educationalists such as the Anti-Racist Teacher Education Network (ARTEN 1986), for presenting the process of compulsory schooling as a non-ideological, non-political and neutral process in which teaching had been designed to meet the 'objective', quantifiable needs of the children. Local CATE committees that were set up had little or no representation from the wider community but were comprised of professionals and representatives of industry and commerce.

Circular 24/89 (DES 1989) replaced the initial accreditation system for the approval of courses in teacher education. This circular strengthened the role of the local committees which were first established by the 1984 Circular with a tighter remit. There is a greater emphasis on business and other outside interests being represented. The government of the day appointed individuals such as Professor Anthony O'Hear (a radical right ideologue and known opponent of teacher education) to CATE. The revised criteria contained in this circular are also far more specific about form and content than is Circular 3/84; for example, there is an increased focus on subject study and the inclusion of technology plus science as a core subject for primary courses. Overall, the changes in the criteria are principally designed to prepare trainees on ITE courses in implementing the requirements of the 1988 Education Reform Act (ERA) and the accompanying National Curriculum.

In terms of equal opportunities, the criteria relating to such matters are still viewed by CATE as concerns to be studied within the educational and professional studies strand, with a continued assertion that pupils need to be prepared for adulthood, citizenship and the world of work within the context of a taken-for-granted, free and civilized society. The criticisms levelled against the criteria in Circular 3/84 remain, but they have even greater validity when we consider that the ERA 1988 has imposed not only the most prescriptive but also arguably a strongly nationalistic curriculum (Cole *et al.* 1990; Davies *et al.* 1990). Despite the limitations of both Circulars 3/84 and 24/89, the influence of CATE on the design and delivery of ITE courses has been considerable. Some ITE institutions were able to argue that equal opportunities issues should not be disregarded but considered as valid areas of study. The guidelines, however, as mentioned above, lacked specificity and thereby allowed institutions to implement the criteria in ways that closely mirrored their own levels of consciousness, prevalent beliefs and levels of competence of staff employed. As a consequence, approaches taken on equality issues are varied and diverse. This was borne out by the evidence cited in (EOC 1989). From a survey of 89 institutions, of which 84 replied, the report found that all respondents duly recognized the importance of gender equality in education and yet 37 per cent of institutions did not have an institutionally specific equal opportunities policy. The investigation further found that where institutions did have a policy there was scant evidence to illustrate how the policies were being implemented and monitored in an effective way. The report states:

> There was considerable disparity between institutions and between departments within institutions on their approach to equal opportunities issues. The best work took place in institutions which had an equal opportunities policy with an associated programme of action which was monitored . . . At the other end of the scale we found indifference and inertia, ad-hocery and a failure to set or evaluate objectives. We found institutions where pockets of exceptionally good work were not known about by those who claimed to represent the institution, and we found equal opportunities policies which were nothing but a paper exercise, but for which substantial claims were made. (EOC 1989, p. 8)

There has not been an equivalent study or national survey undertaken by the CRE, but a limited regional survey was done in the South West by ARTEN (1988). Of 15 institutions contacted, ten replied. All ten had stated rationales in their courses that committed them to the study of issues relating to cultural diversity. Although, as with the EOC survey, they expressed recognition of the importance of studying 'race' and culture issues, there was considerable variation. The survey found that only two institutions out of the ten stated a clear anti-racist rationale. The rest expressed rationales that were clearly multi-cultural/multi-racial or as part of general equal opportunities programme. The survey also found that less than a third of the courses (eight out of 26) had a core input. Four courses offered an option model, while the rest relied, on permeation. Reliance on permeation as an approach to equality issues has serious limitations and because both studies we have quoted examine those shortcomings in considerable detail, we do not propose to rehearse those arguments on these pages.

The latest draft CATE criteria for PGCE (secondary) courses (DES 1992) has departed from previous guidelines by excluding all references to equal opportunities and multi-cultural education. The major thrust of the document is about the shifting of responsibility and resources of ITE from higher education institutions (HEIs) to schools; the acquisition of a narrow set of competencies; and, furthermore, the redefining of teachers from being reflective practitioners to being technicians delivering the narrow requirements of the National Curriculum. The trend towards increasing partnership with schools should be viewed positively. However, we do need to acknowledge that, as in ITE, schools and teachers currently lack the expertise to equip student teachers with the skills and understanding required to recognize factors that disadvantage pupils. This means that when mentors in schools are appointed they need to be provided with full training and support in the issues relating to social justice by the ITE institution concerned. The report on school-based teacher education conducted by HMI (1992, para. vii) states, 'where teachers are given time and training for their role, their contribution to school based training is generally very effective'.

We would endorse this view but would give it even greater credence if the criteria for the selection and subsequent development of mentors included a commitment to develop expertise in the following areas:

a) a clear understanding of the conditions that generate all forms of oppression and consequent strategies and skills needed to counter those oppressions;

b) a sound knowledge of the Race Relations Act 1976 and the Sex Discrimination Act 1975 and the subsequent ability to deal effectively with incidents of racial and sexual harassment;

c) the ability to support the whole language development of multilingual and bidialectical pupils;

d) the ability to develop, deliver and assess formatively the cross-curricular elements of the National Curriculum, in particular those aspects that relate to an understanding of racism, sexism and other oppressions;

e) the ability to make fair and equal judgements and to promote achievement within diverse classrooms.

The proposed criteria intend to abolish local CATE committees. ITE institutions will in future be given CATE approval once every five years. This change to current practice may give individual institutions the autonomy to provide courses to meet the varied and changing needs of schools and also the professional needs of student teachers, without having to seek CATE approval for every innovation and change. However, the need to seek a new mandate every five years may inhibit ITE institutions from adopting radical strategies or designing courses that may incur a rightist backlash from those who seek to maintain the status quo. This has implications for the promotion of equality issues given the total lack of any guidance or reference to equal opportunities in the current criteria.

Modularization

Issues of equality and social justice could be further marginalized by the trend towards modularization of undergraduate ITE courses. Modular degree courses, constituted of free-standing units, are designed to meet the needs of more than one pathway or programme. This flexibility, while effective in terms of unit costs, can structurally exclude modules on equality issues. Where they are included, as compulsory modules, they may be too general and/or too theoretical unless we can ensure that there is a Freirean link between theory and practice (Freire 1972). It is claimed that modularization of ITE courses widens access through the accreditation of prior experience and learning, but this assertion needs to be viewed with a degree of caution, because unless carefully monitored, widening access might simply become a euphemism for increased access to already privileged groups. Compulsory modules which are informed by the concepts and values of equality and social justice perspectives, and which relate to a clear understanding of oppressions, are needed. They must involve analysis and exploration of individuals' social positioning in society and the ways in which this relates to ideologies that impose hierarchies.

In a typical primary teaching degree programme that lasts four years, subject study as specified by CATE criteria which leads to curriculum specialization constitutes 50 per cent of the degree. A further one year is given over for teaching practice. The equivalent of a year that remains of a four-year programme is then left for the study of the compulsory core curriculum subjects plus the other seven National Curriculum foundation subjects. The limited amount of time that remains will be crowded with the study of areas such as classroom organization and management, assessment and record-keeping, teaching and learning styles, and so on. This will leave little if any time within the course for core professional studies to address equality issues. We would in such extreme circumstances, through necessity, propose a model of permeation where the inherent dangers can be avoided by a planned programme of compulsory staff development to ensure that issues relating to racism, sexism and other oppressions are considered as core elements in the development of professional competences required of teachers as reflective practitioners.

An emancipatory (anti-oppression) curriculum for the 1990s

If we are to make progress towards education for social justice, we need to ensure that the structures within institutions are democratic and accountable to staff and students. We must provide student teachers with the skills and understandings necessary to analyse and challenge the structures and processes that oppress them at both the personal level and within the wider social dimension of groups and communities which are subjugated and disfranchised to perpetuate a hierarchy of power and privilege. In the context of teacher education, this must include an understanding of the structures and purposes of the institution itself.

The rationale and course objectives of an ITE curriculum in an HEI, like any other programme provided by that institution, have to be measured against its mission statement and statement of shared values. Its rationale and course objectives should include the development of people's creative potential and an understanding of the natural world, of the society in which we live and of the work processes of that society. It should be concerned with the development of the capacity to work with others in the shaping of society's future beyond narrow national interests. However, mission statements are invariably based on the premise that there is a shared understanding of concepts such as fairness/unfairness and bias/objectivity that are clearly located in the notion that all HEIs are liberal and humanistic. This model of equality of opportunity may even recognize the pluralist democracy that we live in. It may, furthermore, take the view that discrimination on the grounds of 'race' or gender is unlawful, certainly immoral, but this model locks people into viewing inequalities manifested on a personal level with prejudice, discrimination and harassment as inevitable consequences. This focus on the behavioural aspects of individuals or groups reinforces the view of racism and sexism as unacceptable aberrant behaviour.

Student teachers need the skills to explore the ways in which knowledge, as constructed and structured, contributes towards the legitimation of inequalities and oppressions. The existence of hierarchies in terms of subjects, and, furthermore, what content within those subjects constitutes 'valued knowledge', is itself circumscribed by the patriarchy and its dominant cultural values. We therefore need to equip students with the intellectual skills to examine critically the nature of the curriculum so that they can in turn consider and challenge the ideologies that underpin the selection of knowledge that they are being asked to acquire and teach through the National Curriculum. Subject studies can no longer be seen as sacrosanct areas of the ITE programme. Tutors in these areas must acknowledge the responsibility they have in ensuring that their subject provides students with the opportunity to develop a critical attitude to the social, political and economic consequences in the application of that knowledge. Knowledge and skills acquired should not serve the purpose of simply reproducing current hegemonic structures. Course management should include an audit of learning outcomes that requires evidence that these critical skills have been developed and applied by student teachers.

As part of the institutional structures, tutors engage in the certification process to produce a teacher that can be ranked and awarded a high-level credential. Our role as gatekeepers to the world of employment enables us to exercise considerable power over student teachers and exact a level of compliance on their part. The whole process of certification and ranking maintains a meritocracy of triumphant individualism.

We need to consider the extent to which students are included in the planning of the curriculum. Course Boards and Boards of Study usually have student representatives, but their role in the management of the programme is often limited. The method of electing representatives and defining their rights and responsibilities needs to be considered urgently. Working parties that are currently overseeing the implementation and management of mentorship programmes should have student representation to ensure that partnership with schools is forged on the basis of shared principles and values. Furthermore, ITE institutions need to take a lead in ensuring that these are underpinned by a commitment to social justice through equality (Clay *et al.* 1991, p. 29). This will also help to counteract the development of a culture of 'conflict avoidance' that leads to a model of 'stasis' as outlined by Menter (1989) in writing about the ITE school experience partnership.

The only credible basis for the promotion and achievement of an anti-oppression curriculum is through the development of a 'holistic' view of social justice issues by recognizing all forms of oppression and not allowing 'experts' to colonize areas and establish hierarchies, through partnership between students and tutors who express a desire to see social justice and equality in education achieving primacy. The development of an open forum on social justice where students and staff (teaching and non-teaching) can meet in a supportive environment is a possible way forward where individual self-development comes through the sharing of experience and ideas, with tutors contributing their knowledge not by 'transmission teaching' but through interlocution, where individual contributions are valued and respected. The culture of the open forum must foster a climate in which individual levels of consciousness, understandings and experiences are legitimated. The position of tutors within the hierarchy gives them greater access to information which can be pooled to provide students with 'pathways into the labyrinth'.

The creation of such a forum has been written about by one of the authors (Clay *et al.* 1991).

Finally, and most importantly, the strategies we advocate are based on the premise that it is only when student teachers are equipped to recognize oppression and develop strategies to challenge them that they will in turn feel confident and able to educate pupils to combat oppression. Baker (1987, pp. 151–2) says that

> [a]nyone who takes equality seriously has to take seriously a commitment to egalitarian politics. By definition, that politics has to oppose *racism* and *sexism* . . . it must also be socialist in the broad sense of prompting a *democratically* planned economy . . . what matters is seeing that equality without politics is impossible. But equality is not an end in itself: it only matters because of its effect on people's lives . . . and how we relate to each other in 'private' either supports or challenges the way power and privilege are structured in society as a whole . . . equality is concerned not just with the structure of whole societies, but with human relationships in general. No one person can change the whole world. But each of us can make a start – if only by arguing for equality.

References

ARTEN (1986) *Anti-Racist Teacher Education*, Occasional Papers 1–3, Jordanhill College, Glasgow.

ARTEN (1988) *Permeation: The Road to Nowhere*, Jordanhill College of Education, Glasgow.

Baker, J. (1987) *Arguing for Equality*, Verso, London.

Clay, J. and Cole, M. (1991) 'General principles for a socialist agenda in education for the 1990s and into the twenty first century' in C. Chitty (ed.), *Changing the Future: Redprint for Education*, Tufnell Press, London, pp. 1–14.

Clay, J., Gadhia, S. and Wilkins, C. (1991) 'Racism and institutional inertia: a 3-D perspective of initial teacher education (disillusionment, disaffection and despair)', *Multicultural Teaching*, vol. 9, no. 3.

Cole, M., Clay, J. and Hill, D. (1990) 'The citizen as "individual" and nationalist or "social" and internationalist? What is the role of education?', *Critical Social Policy*, no. 30, Winter.

Davies, A.M., Holland. J. and Minhas, R. (1990) *Equal Opportunities in the New ERA*, Tufnell Press, London.

DES (1984) *Initial Teacher Training: Approval of Courses*, Circular No. 3/84, 13 April, HMSO, London.

DES (1989) *Initial Teacher Training: Approval of Courses*, Circular No. 24/89, HMSO.

DES (1992) *Reform of Initial Teacher Training: A Consultative Document*, HMSO, London.

Equal Opportunities Commission (1989) *Formal Investigation Report: Initial Teacher Training in England and Wales*, EOC, Manchester.

Freire, P. (1972) *Pedagogy of the Oppressed*, Penguin, London.

HMI (1992) *School Based Teacher Education: A Report*, DES, London.

ILEA (1985) *Policy for Equality*, ILEA, London.

Menter, I. (1989) 'Teaching practice stasis: racism, sexism and school experience in initial teacher education', *British Journal of Sociology of Education*, vol. 10, no. 4.

CHAPTER 10

From Rhetoric to Reality: Strategies for Developing a Social Justice Approach to Educational Decision-Making

LEONE BURTON and GABY WEINER

In this chapter, we suggest strategies which may make places such as schools, teacher and other higher education institutions more comfortable and equitable places in which to study and work. Some of our suggestions come from our own experiences as teachers, researchers and managers in a variety of education sectors, although we also draw on the findings of a project in which we were both involved.

Educational institutions, especially schools and local education authorities, were amongst the first to develop policies in the area of equal opportunities. By the mid-1980s, some LEAs, for example Berkshire, the Inner London Education Authority and Brent, required individual institutions to develop explicit equal opportunities policies around 'race', class and gender which enabled them to confront and challenge inequalities in their structures and in their practice. Many of these have continued to develop policy and practice in this area, while others have been less energetic, as the recent annual report of Her Majesty's Chief Inspector of Schools reveals:

Progress on equal opportunities is best described as patchy. In

some schools and colleges, awareness of the take-up of educational opportunities as between the sexes and among ethnic
minorities is high; in other areas it is totally inadequate. Most
institutions have policies for promoting equality of opportunity
but too often the gap between policy and practice is unacceptably
wide. (HMI 1992, p. 7)

During the same period, restructuring in education and
economic and demographic changes have led educational institutions to reconsider not only their roles as *providers* of educational opportunities but also their *responsibilities* to their local
communities. It was in this climate that funding for a project was
gained for the study of the lives and experiences of senior
managers from under represented groups in educational
institutions.

For this project (reported in Powney and Weiner 1991) 'life-
history' interviews were conducted with 40 women and black
and ethnic minority managers in educational institutions with
the main aims of exploring their career strategies and the personal and institutional obstacles they experienced, and identifying management strategies that might enhance the promotion of
men and women from similarly under represented groups.

The project was initiated in order to challenge the still white,
male preserve of educational management even though, as we
have seen, equal opportunities policies are being increasingly
promoted as appropriate for modern educational institutions of
the 1990s (Crabb 1987; Feather and Russell 1990; Taylor 1990).
One way forward, it seemed, was to consult the small number
of existing women and black and ethnic minority managers
about their experiences and suggestions for reducing the current
imbalance. We thus interviewed a range of senior personnel
across all education sectors including headteachers, principals
and deputies in further and higher education, senior academics,
administrators, inspectors and advisers. Roughly three-quarters
of our interviewees were women, two thirds of whom were
white; and black men and black women each constituted about
a quarter of the overall number of interviewees. We used a life-
history approach (Mies 1983) because we hoped it would enable
us to explore the obstacles confronting individuals as well as to
identify key issues which would provide the basis for institutional policy change.

While we are critical of existing hierarchical management structures and the increasing managerialism creeping into educational institutions, this chapter focuses on what can be done *now* rather than arguing for a complete transformation of managerial practice. The latter is long overdue but needs greater time and space than is available here. Nevertheless, in suggesting strategies and institutional interventions which we anticipate will promote more equitable practices, we are aware of the 'micro-politics' of institutions (Ball 1987) which render complex any change, particularly concerning power relations. Thus, as MacIntyre (1985, p. 106) suggests, changes made within organizations cannot be guaranteed to produce the anticipated or desired outcomes: 'Since organisational success and organisational predictability exclude one another, the project of creating a wholly or largely predictable organisation committed to a wholly or largely predictable society is doomed and doomed by the facts about social life.' Despite much of the literature on management implying the contrary, and however carefully plans are developed at management level, outcomes will be unpredictable. There is even tacit agreement about this, according to Hoyle (1988, p. 255): 'everyone working in organisations is all too well aware of their often idiosyncratic, adventitious, unpredictable and intractable nature when every day brings a new organisational "pathology"' to disrupt well laid plans. Nevertheless, we suggest that there are strategies which will encourage greater equality in the workplace, and that careful planning is important if any change is to be achieved. Five strategies emerged from the life-history research described above which we wish to explore further: mentoring; consultative management style; supportive ambience; networking; and institutional stance.

Mentoring

In the educational world, mentoring has recently achieved notoriety because of the way it has been developed within teacher education. For example, it was suggested by Kenneth Clark, the former Minister for Education, that student teachers should receive most of their training on the job from 'mentors'

– experienced teachers with special responsibility for trainee teachers. In his speech to the North of England Education Conference in January 1992, he said: 'I find the concept of the "mentor" teacher with a particular responsibility for a student or group of students an attractive one' (para. 25).

To date, however, there has been little clarification about how this mentoring is to be accomplished, what training the mentors themselves require and in what aspects, and the anticipated relationship between mentor and mentee. Other systems of mentoring have a longer history.

Mentoring has been used formally in industry and commerce, and informally in most parts of the public and private sectors. In analysing the information collected for our research, it became clear that the notion of mentoring is neither simple nor uniform. Interviewees frequently mentioned mentoring either with respect to actual mentors or to particular people who had been significant to career development. For example, a black female manager reported that

> the Head of Department was a mentor to me. He constantly offered de-briefing on my lessons and classroom skills. If one is open to it, I find mentoring systems very effective.[1]

Another interviewee, this time a white manager, remembered that

> my non-managerial supervisor was very challenging, would never let me off the hook, would not let me say it was my fault and never let me leave her house in pieces but would put me back together again.

Yet another white female manager identified her boss as a key figure in her career. He was a Director of Education who:

> provided an example of someone who could have a strong influence on education, get involved in political policy issues and I took to it like a duck to water. He pointed out that if I was going to achieve my full potential there were certain things that I must do and he very kindly kept a benevolent eye on my career from then onwards. If it hadn't been for him I would not have had that strong thrust in the right direction and the depth and breadth of experience. He made sure that I had a grounding in some of the things that people coming straight in from teaching don't often have.

For a black male manager, his multi-cultural adviser was important:

> During my early career, I worked closely with the multi-cultural advisor who was a key person in my career. When he moved on, I applied for and got his position.

These were the positive experiences. But many of our participants had negative experiences of racism and sexism which were initiated at the work or study place where the existence of a mentor might have been at the least a support or, more ambitiously, an instrument of challenge and change. From our study, it became evident that there were at least four approaches to mentoring.

One-off mentoring

This takes place at a single session in which advice, information or support is offered by one individual to another. Pre-briefing sessions might well fall into this category, providing an opportunity for an interview candidate to rehearse and consider his/her responses to the kinds of question which might well arise at an interview. At the simplest level, this can help to counter interview nerves, but it can also encourage candidates to reconsider the demands and requirements of the role for which they are applying. It can provoke a form of reflection that brings out any strengths for the post and particular reasons for applying. Similarly, de-briefing sessions can provide single opportunities to evaluate performance after an interview, identifying shortcomings and deciding on actions that will strengthen future applications. Much of the information which is appropriate to one-off mentoring sessions is of the kind which should be dealt with in appraisal; but there is accumulating evidence that appraisal does not necessarily function in this way for certain groups. For example, gender issues in teacher appraisal have drawn critical comments from Chisholm (1988) and Myers (1989), while Barbour (1991) has produced anecdotal evidence on gender difference in appraisal in the university sector.

Senior-to-junior mentoring

This is a system whereby an experienced member of staff becomes an 'institutional friend' to a newcomer who is often located in another section of the organization. Overtly transforming the 'old boy network' so that its advantages can be experienced by all, this provides access to the institutional ethos and support to the newcomer who can question and challenge structures without becoming embroiled in the complications of existing departmental hierarchies. Induction incorporating a mentoring system of this kind can create a supportive and friendly cross-departmental work environment for a new recruit.

Colleague-to-colleague mentoring

Here, members of staff of equivalent levels of seniority, one established and the other new, are deliberately partnered for a fixed period of time. Again, the intention is to induct the new member of staff into the ethos and style of the institution as equitably as is possible.

An alternative colleague-to-colleague mentoring system includes hierarchy within it: for example, a senior colleague mentoring a junior colleague or, in the case of possible future teacher education changes, an experienced teacher mentoring a student teacher. We have noticed that student teachers often report after teaching practice that some class teachers offer more to students than supervision. Those who mentor are described as the most helpful in terms of student learning and success.

However, such a notion of mentoring neither emerged from our study nor is visible in the literature. In essence, it conflicts with the view of a mentor as being a professional 'friend' or 'guide' by introducing an element of supervision, and consequently, an assessment of professional competence.

In our view, such potential conflicts are likely to be unhelpful to both mentor and mentee. If, however, such colleague-to-colleague mentoring is to be used, relationships need to be clearly defined, so that each party understands the nature of the relationship and so that the possibility of abuse is minimized. These issues are relevant to recent school-base developments in initial teacher education where mentoring schemes, conscious of the needs of black and female students, will need to be established with collaborating schools.

Internal–external mentoring

This involves members of an institution in adopting prospective future incomers in order to demystify the institution. Such procedures have been successfully adopted in the United States; for example, in order to encourage consideration of a university education, black and ethnic minority pupils are partnered with university students. The aim is to replace myth and vulnerability with information and experience. While such policies can assist access, they cannot be guaranteed to provide continued support once university entrance has been gained. 'Maintenance' is more likely to be achieved by internal mentoring and networking.

Management style

It became evident, early in our research, that most of our interviewees were aiming for a more 'democratic' management style than is currently visible in educational institutions; moreover, those with a particular concern to promote equal opportunities within their institution saw the process of democratizing structures as part of the necessary changes. A black male manager, for example, described his management style as:

> consultative . . . and well rooted in democratic principles

and a white female manager took it for granted that

> everyone wants to be involved and participate in decision-making . . . [and] that decisions won't be made without consultation.

Alongside these values, sustaining and encouraging less senior colleagues from under represented groups is also important. One white female manager reported being particularly alert to the needs of female staff: she

> deliberately nurtures and has a tendency . . . to provide stronger

support and encouragement to young women because she is aware of the obstacles in their path to promoting their career.

Certainly, being aware of equal opportunities issues and how they may be reflected in dealing with staff, for example, in interviews, training, adequate representation in a range of roles at different levels of seniority, and on all work teams and committees, seems crucial.

'Openness' is another characteristic of this management approach: it enables managers to get to know the people with whom they are working and also prevents them becoming, as one interviewee put it, 'bogged down' in paper work. 'Being seen around' and being accessible to both staff and pupils and/or students is therefore high on the agenda, as is showing respect to and valuing the contributions of staff and students at whatever level. The utilization of team and committee structures to share out work and decision-making is central to the work of a democratic manager. As one interviewee said:

decisions are taken jointly [and there is] collective ownership [of] success and failure.

The manager's role is multi-dimensional: offering combinations of leadership, counselling, appraisal and advice to colleagues – both personally and professionally.

One of the difficulties, however, is how to handle conflict. Many of our interviewees were self-critical about uncertainty in this area; and it is more difficult, we suggest, when decision-making is diffuse and leadership is shared. Any challenge to the manager's authority tends to be more complex, overt, and perhaps more personally threatening than in a more authoritarian managerial structure. Another difficulty is the possibility of 'burn-out', as the importance and stress of nurturing and sustaining relationships adopted by this management approach needs to be accommodated alongside the heavy bureaucratic workload of most senior managers.

Also, if institutions have a genuine commitment to extending equality, they need to recognize that black and/or female managers may face additional problems to those of their white and/or male counterparts. One of our interviewees reported experiences of deliberate attempts at sabotage:

[she] is aware that there are some staff who deliberately set out

to undermine her using subtle strategies such as questioning every decision she makes, preferring to consult with white managers about areas of work which directly come under her brief.

Another claimed that there has to be a difference in management style between black and white managers:

> In some ways there has to be a difference. A black manager managing both black and white staff has particular difficulties. · His experience has been that white staff are constantly watching how he manages black staff and black staff watching how he manages white staff and both watching how he manages both sets of staff together. For white managers this dynamic does not necessarily exist in the same way . . . He feels that he is constantly being watched to see whether or not he can manage.

The twin disadvantages of being both a woman and black were illustrated thus:

> black women managers have to be twice as good because they are women and twice as good because they are black.

The point being made here is that while it is important to develop sound management practices and a clear structure, institutions wishing to encourage more equitable practices among their members must themselves see that social justice practices permeate senior levels. Treatment of senior managers needs to reflect equal opportunities approaches throughout each institution – tinkering with appointments procedures is not enough! An equal opportunities policy needs both to permeate all institutional structures and to develop strategies for ensuring its maintenance. The development of recognition, within an educational institution, of the social justice implications of adopting and implementing different management styles leads to the encouragement of, for example, informal and formal networks for sharing experiences and exchanging information on the adoption of mentoring strategies.

Ambience

The workplace ethos of educational institutions is important not only for those who are employed there but for those who attend as learners. If the ethos is friendly and welcoming, with structures deliberately created to offer support and encouragement to individuals, new entrants, whether for work or study, will react very differently. Many of our interviewees emphasized the importance of creating a welcoming environment, say, for black or female students, and were critical of institutions which appear to be failing to listen to what people tell them about the ethos that they project. In a highly competitive environment, such failure can prove very costly.

The changes that might be made include alternative avenues for advertising for staff and/or students and using language that is accessible. Attending to the manner with which enquiries are dealt and how visitors are welcomed are also important. In an educational institution, for example, how can the ethos be improved in the foyer, in the manner of contact between staff and visitor, in displays, and so on? Who is seen to be of value and how?

The common response to failure to recruit from under-represented groups – that applications are not forthcoming – is, in our view, only the tip of the institutional iceberg. It is certainly the case that positions advertised externally in the 'usual' newspapers and journals do not attract substantial applications from underrepresented groups. However, experiences reported individually and institutionally to the project team suggest that lack of interest is unlikely to be the major cause. Qualified people are neither likely to regard themselves as appropriate employees nor recognize the institution as an appropriate workplace if they feel they are unlikely to be welcome or comfortable there.

A policy of *active search* can be instituted. This requires that a short-list which continues to represent the current imbalance is unacceptable, thus putting the onus on the institution to search for appropriate and representative personnel at all times – not only when a post becomes available. It also requires that staff policies are framed to generate the kind of experiences which help to create an appropriate profile for those staff from under-represented groups who have promotion potential. In the case of one university in Canada which has such a policy of active search, the short-list for a post of nuclear physicist drawn up by a department was unacceptable because it contained only male applicants. By utilizing networks, the university approached a highly qualified woman who originated from the city in which the university was located but who lived and worked elsewhere. She had been unaware of the vacancy, was encouraged to apply through the usual procedures of the appointing committee, and got the job!

Recruitment is often a contentious area. A serious attempt to change the 'race' and sex distribution of staff and students requires the consideration of different strategies to those usually chosen. This may mean looking for people with a different range of experience and fields which are akin to, but not precisely the same as, those usually chosen. The interviewing process may need to be rearranged to reflect the experiences and expectations of the post or the course rather than those of the interviewers. One way of making the institutional position on equal opportunities clear to the local community and of demonstrating the value that is placed on close collaboration is to involve representatives from local black and ethnic minority groups in institutional developments – as members of committees or of interview panels for appointments and/or entry on to courses. This not only acknowledges the existence of institutional racism and sexism but also draws on the wealth of local knowledge and expertise to help the institution overcome any lack of representation. (See also Chapter 8.)

It is also worth emphasizing that there is little to be gained by recruiting members of underrepresented groups if nothing is done about the ambience of the institution or changing other structures. In this case, the institution will rely upon individuals to use their energies to push for change – a racist and sexist expectation, we believe – and 'burn-out' or alienation will be the result. And ultimately, the white, male dominance of the institution will remain – enshrined in its structures and uncontested practices.

Networking

Networking, whether formally organized or informally arranged by the network members themselves, has been uniformly praised by those who have experienced its benefits. A black female interviewee gave the example of how, within an institution, formal networking can be initiated:

the chief inspector initiated meetings among the black inspectors who formed a caucus which provided a sense of solidarity and strength. Many still remain close friends.

Another, this time white, female manager reported that she had begun:

> a women's network which continues to be very strong and supportive. Out of that developed a national network on which I continue to rely. Once you lay out a set of principles and a philosophy to which men also subscribe, they join the network and I think that is important. Some people 'knock' successful women who therefore also need network support.

The importance of networking was further identified by a black male manager thus:

> I benefited from being a member of the Black Teachers' Support Group as it brought me into contact with other colleagues who are able to understand the pressures of being a black headteacher.

Loss of network faced another interviewee who remembered feelings of isolation on moving to a new job:

> I had to settle to a new city, new job, new home and felt cut off from my networks.

Networking has long been used as a means of mutual professional reinforcement; the successes of masonic lodges and the 'old boy network' are widely recognized. Networking as a means of extending solidarity within less powerful groups has a shorter history; yet it has already proved extremely valuable at both staff and student level. It can encourage mutual support, shared expertise and advice when in difficulty. As more members of underrepresented groups experience the benefits of networking, the use of networks is bound to grow informally even if discouraged institutionally. However, it is as well that institutions are aware of the ways in which such networks can provide them with valuable information which can, in turn, contribute to the ongoing implementation of equal opportunities policies. Regular meetings between senior management and network members are one way of alerting the institution to inequalities which can be resolved, to the most effective form of remedial action, and to the existence of qualified future employees or employees currently being underutilized.

Institutional stance

Our research indicated that there are various levels of institutional commitment towards equal opportunities, and that these are related to the perceived status of educational institutions. Lower-status institutions such as schools, adult and further education and the youth service appear to have a greater commitment to equal opportunities because of the multi-racial and less privileged constituencies that they often serve or because, as much smaller more intimate and cohesive institutions, staff members may have a more sympathetic perspective on equality issues. In the past, pressure from committed education authorities has led to increased activity related to equal opportunities. Currently, 'market' needs appear to be stimulating similar interest more broadly.

Institutional stance towards equal opportunities varied, in our research, from no evidence of any awareness or adherence to equal opportunities issues (which we termed 'apathy'), through working towards equal opportunities (termed 'predisposition'), through to commitment to equal opportunities shaping the entire institutional ethos and structure (termed 'ethos'). In the last case, this is characterized by a comparatively high number of staff and students from underrepresented groups which are proportionally represented at senior management levels. Particularly important in the management structures of such institutions are: carefully developed and implemented recruitment, appointment and promotion procedures; targeted staff development and training programmes focusing, in particular, on staff from underrepresented groups; effective appraisal systems, sensitive to the differing lives and career patterns of staff members; explicit equal opportunities policies which are well publicized, monitored and lead to changes in policy; policies on student access which take into account life experiences as well as formal qualifications and which offer support throughout a course rather than merely at the point of entry; initiatives that favour the recruitment and retention of female staff and students such as childcare provision, flexitime studying and working, flexible study and work-packages and fast-track career development.

Conclusion

Black and ethnic minority men and women are still hard to find in senior management positions in educational institutions in the UK. Although more visible, white women are also under-represented, even where they numerically dominate the workforce, for example as primary teachers. Thus, there are currently more male heads and deputy heads of schools, inspectors, senior/principal lecturers, readers and professors; and to date, there is no university vice-chancellor who breaks the white, male norm (see, for example, publications from the Equal Opportunities Commission (EOC), and SCRE 1992).

At the same time, able people from a variety of under-represented groups are being inhibited from making their contribution to the educational service, often as a consequence of institutionalized racism and sexism. Instead, they have to contend with the demands of establishing themselves in a career at the same time as being disadvantaged by the prejudices of their colleagues or by institutional structures. It seems to us that, from both an economic and a social justice perspective, there is an urgent need to shift from rhetoric to reality and from policy to practice.

In this chapter, then, we have drawn attention to five different areas which can be seen as mechanisms for inducing change: mentoring; management style; institutional ambience; networking; and institutional profile. They fall into two groups. Institutional ambience and profile are amenable to senior management policy decision-making that relates to the physical environment and the behaviour of those within it. We have highlighted a number of possibilities where change can be effected relatively easily and speedily.

Mentoring and networking, on the other hand, are interpersonal support mechanisms and, even if instigated within an institutional policy framework, are dependent on the commitment and skill of those involved. A reluctant mentor may well be more harmful than no mentor at all. Mentors will need training so as to be more responsive to longer-term strategies (including equal opportunities) in which both institutional and personal behaviour are acknowledged as centrally important.

Management style cuts across institutional and personal

factors. The different management styles identified in the literature as 'masculine' and 'feminine' or 'hierarchical' and 'collaborative' (see, for example, Marshall 1985; Woo 1985; Barsoux 1987; and Al-Khalifa 1989) carry with them implications and expectations which have social justice dimensions. Interestingly, in our project, most white female and black male managers espoused a democratic management style – black female managers appeared to adopt a more directive 'leadership' approach. The project report concluded that it might be easier to get things done by offering strong leadership or 'pulling rank' if uncertain of one's acceptance by subordinates (Powney and Weiner 1991, p. 43). Clearly, preferred management style is related not only to the value system of the manager, but also to his/her status position within the organization and to current and previous experiences of workplace ethos.

These findings suggest, in our view, that individuals and institutions need to become more reflective about their styles of management and the impact these might have on performance. Choosing to use a particular style for a particular purpose, and having a range from which to choose, seems to us to be more empowering than merely adopting a stance because it feels 'comfortable', is consistent with previous practice or apparently suits one's personality.

We are not suggesting that there is a management style 'solution' to every problem. However, the managers in our project provide very useful 'pointers' from their own experiences. They were helped and encouraged by others; responded better to open and collaborative rather than hierarchical and closed management approaches; benefited in their careers from explicit equal opportunities policies; and believed that clarity about roles and responsibilities was crucial to equitable institutional practice.

We now have some 'equity' strategies – it will be interesting to see if, and how they are put into practice – and whether, eventually, they have any impact on the existing unequal distribution of senior management posts.

Note

1 Direct quotes from project field notes and interviews are set indented.

References

Al-Khalifa, E. (1989) 'Management by halves – Women teachers and school management' in H. De Lyon and F. Widdowson Migniuolo (eds), *Women Teachers: Issues and Experience*, Open University Press, Milton Keynes.

Ball, S.J. (1987) *The Micro-politics of the School: Towards a Theory of School Organisation*, Methuen, London.

Barbour, L. (1991), *AUT Woman*, 23.

Barsoux, J.L., (1987) 'From dinner jacket to straight jacket – what kind of manager does industry need?', *Times Educational Supplement*, 17 July, p. 13.

Chisholm, L. (1988) 'Teachers' work appraisal and gender'. Paper presented to the International Sociology of Education Conference, Westhill College, Birmingham.

Crabb, S. (1987) 'Results of a questionnaire on equal pay policy', *Women in Further and Higher Education Management*, Report, Coombe Lodge.

EOC (1991) *Some Facts about Women 1991*, EOC, Manchester.

Feather, D. and Russell, S. (1990) 'A management course for women teachers', *Women in Management*, vol. 5, no. 5, pp. 7–10.

HMI (1992) *Education in England 1990–91: Annual Report of HM Senior Chief Inspector of Schools*, HMSO, London.

Hoyle, E. (1987) 'Micropolitics of educational organisations' in A. Westoby (ed.), *Culture and Power in Educational Organizations*, Open University Press, Milton Keynes.

MacIntyre, A. (1985) *After Virtue: A Study in Moral Theory*, Duckworth, London.

Marshall, C. (1985) 'From culturally defined to self defined: career stages of women administrators', *Journal of Educational Thought*, vol. 19, no. 2, pp. 134–47.

Mies, M., (1983) 'Towards a methodology for feminist research' in G. Bowles and R. Duelli Klein (eds), *Theories of Women's Studies*, Routledge and Kegan Paul, London.

Myers, K. (1989), 'High heels in the market place', *Education*, June, pp. 559–60.

Powney, J. and Weiner, G. (1991) *'Outside of the Norm': Equity and*

Management in Educational Institutions: Project Report, London, South Bank Polytechnic, London.

Scottish Council for Research in Education (SCRE) (1992) 'A note on some statistical gender differences in Scottish education', *SCRE Newsletter*, 50, Spring, pp. 7–8.

Taylor, H. (1990) 'Management development for black teachers', *Women in Management*, vol. 5, no. 5, pp. 15–17.

Woo, L.C. (1985) 'Women administrators: profiles of success', *Phi Delta Kappa*, vol. 67, no. 4, pp. 285–8.

CHAPTER 11

Developing Equality through Local Education Authority INSET

PRATAP DESHPANDE and NARGIS RASHID

Background

It is widely accepted that initial teacher education (ITE) cannot provide all the knowledge and skills that teachers will need during their careers. In the context of education for equality this is particularly applicable as the ability of teachers to deal with issues of 'race' and gender will be strongly influenced by a range of variables over which they have varying degrees of influence or control. Strategies that are successful in one context do not always translate to other contexts. The 'tools' that teachers need include their own awareness of issues as well as their choice of strategy to manage the change process in a school. The pertinent range of INSET provision is therefore as wide as the full range available. Every aspect of professional development carries with it implications for 'race' and gender equality and the potential to enhance that equality.

Local education authorities (LEAs) have been principal providers of professional development for teachers. The introduction of 'teacher days' and the allocation of grants for professional development from the Department of Education and Science (now the Department for Education (DFE)) have shown recognition of the need for continued teacher education and enabled schools and LEAs to plan for this in a coherent way to meet both local and national priorities. Many LEAs and schools have made positive use of LEA Training Grants and Education Support Grants to develop practice and enhance equality in education for children of ethnic minority backgrounds and to educate all children for our multi-cultural society. Such work has been greatly assisted by the fact that LEAs were able to bid for grants which were available for these specific purposes.

Changing roles and potential

Education has become an increasingly high-profile political issue over the last two decades. A high level of public interest and concern, allied to a governmental recognition of a need for change to maximize the potential of the population and to meet the challenges and opportunities of a unifying European market, has led to enormous changes in education which are not yet complete. Initiatives in teacher education to increase the recruitment from ethnic minority groups have parallels in other careers. It is open to question whether the initiatives are driven by a desire to create equal opportunities or merely the result of a recognition of an untapped pool in a climate of shortages in supply.

In the context of the role of LEA INSET, the principal changes and their effects are summarized below:

1 The Education Act (No. 2) of 1986 transferred the prime responsibility for schools away from LEAs to governing bodies. This shift of responsibility and power has been greatly increased by the Local Management of Schools introduced by the Education Reform Act of 1988. This has clearly made the training for governors particularly important.

2 The definition of an entitlement curriculum through the introduction of the National Curriculum has resulted in an enormous focusing of the time and energy of teachers as implementation stages are reached. The need for a permeation has therefore become especially urgent to ensure that the enhancement of equality and the addressing of issues of 'race' and gender are seen to be essential to the implementation of the National Curriculum.

3 The inspection of the quality of education and the public reporting of the achievements of pupils are both required by the Education (Schools) Act of 1992 and will have a significant effect upon the priority given to the issues of 'race' and gender in schools.

4 The disappearance of specific national priority categories dealing with 'race' within GEST and the high level of devolution of grants to schools will have considerable effects upon strategies LEAs and schools can use to provide and access appropriate INSET.

The changes summarized above are only a selection from those that have, or soon will, impact upon education. They show a clear thrust to increase public accountability and to enhance educational quality.

In this chapter we essentially set out the features of three particular approaches within our LEA which have been used during the last five years and which offer potential for LEA INSET in addressing education for equality. They share features in common, some aspects are direct evolutions of earlier approaches in other LEAs, and they show incremental growth and learning within our LEA. Importantly, they all offer features which are appropriate and potentially powerful within the current context for education.

They are briefly described below, though without the full contextualization to show how they fitted into the fuller LEA strategy due to the space available within this chapter. They are:

- Education for Our Multicultural Society: the Delivery Strategy for Schools (MC), 1987-9;
- Quality Development in Schools (QD), from 1990;
- Training for Governing Bodies (GT), from 1989.

Education for our multicultural society: the delivery strategy for schools

In the academic year 1986-7, when MC was designed, it was already known that the role and responsibilities of school governors were going to be increasingly important. In particular, it was important to use an approach which would help governing bodies to use the LEA policies to formulate their own. The LEA had already adopted a policy in 1981, and reaffirmed it in 1984, for 'Education in our Multicultural Society', in all its institutions. It had (and has) three aims:

- to be aware of and counter racism and the discriminatory practices to which it gives rise;

- to be aware of and provide for the particular needs of pupils having regard for their ethnic, cultural, historical, linguistic and religious backgrounds;
- to prepare all pupils for life in our multi-cultural society, and build upon the strengths of cultural diversity.

It was also recognized that there was a need to focus the efforts within schools to enhance the achievement of ethnic minority pupils through the implementation of the aims. Clearly the features within schools that can impact on achievement are many. Our approach identified the features as those through which pupils saw themselves as valued (or not) and which had effect on their achievement. These features were:

- the selection of knowledge for the curriculum;
- the use made of all the pupil's knowledge for learning;
- teaching and learning materials for display;
- the content of, and presenters at, assemblies;
- careers guidance/education, including the early formation of aspirations;
- the nature of the partnership with parents;
- the relationships between pupils, teachers and pupils and between teachers;
- the learning potential in activities and tasks;
- the range of teaching styles;
- the grouping of pupils into classes and within classes;
- the procedures for assessment;
- the use of rewards and sanctions;
- the pastoral care;
- the staffing structure, the recruitment and development opportunities for staff;
- the governing body, its membership and activities.

The delivery model was based on the conviction that the ownership of self-sustaining change in a school was best achieved by ensuring that pupil and parental perceptions were taken into account by teachers and that the teachers would be best enskilled by being the developers themselves. This model for change is well supported by the experience of a number of LEAs and other organizations engaged in curriculum and professional development. The delivery had the following key features.

A Training and Development Unit (TDU) of teachers was set

up drawing on the expertise of support teachers within the LEA's Multicultural Support Service. This service was partly funded by a grant from the Home Office under Section 11 of the Local Government Act 1966. The members of TDU received a ten-day course, largely from LEA advisers, to help them to refine their skills in monitoring and evaluating the planned and received curriculum, in gaining and using the perceptions of ethnic minority parents, in revising and reconstructing the curriculum to maximize the potential for achievement and working with teachers in a way that supported and facilitated (rather than led or dictated) the developments.

Schools were invited to take part in a two-year programme which aimed at enhancing ethnic minority pupil achievement and educated all pupils for our multicultural society. The response was very encouraging and included schools which had few or no pupils of ethnic minority backgrounds. Forty-four nursery, primary, secondary and special schools with high numbers of ethnic minority pupils joined the programme. Each school was invited to nominate a senior teacher who would receive a ten-day course provided by the TDU, with some inputs from advisers and ethnic minority parents. The course was similar to that received by the TDU. The tasks included the analysis of practice in the participant's own school. The senior teachers became the lead facilitators in their schools.

Headteachers from the participating schools were provided with two-day conferences by advisers to help them analyse the implications for change in their schools in the light of the policy and in the context of the effects of the changing role of governing bodies and the Education Reform Bill of 1987 which became an Act in 1988. The conferences recognized the changing relationship between LEAs and schools and therefore sought to help headteachers in their own development planning and management of change to reach objectives that they set within the aims of the programme. The way in which responsibilities were located in the schools, where they properly belonged, and the supportive role of the LEA were central to the approach and this is one of the reasons why there is much in the approach which is still applicable in 1992 and in the likely future.

The lead facilitators began their work in their schools by

ensuring that all staff (in many schools this included the non-teaching staff) were made aware of the rationale and nature of proposed developmental work and were able to receive the concerns and perspectives of ethnic minority parents directly. The importance of including all stakeholders in prioritizing development targets was well taken by schools and there were many examples of governor and parental involvement and some of pupil involvement. The lead facilitators led working groups of teachers, typically of about four, to work on the development prioritized by the school. This work was assisted by a support teacher from the TDU or the Multicultural Support Service in its analytic, planning, implementation and evaluation stages.

Typically, support teachers worked with two schools. Schools moved on to their succeeding priorities, at a pace dictated by the target, with a different working group retaining some of the members of the previous group so that the dissemination of experience was possible in a very practical way. The targets chosen by the schools during the two-year period were interesting in that some schools anticipated some of the issues that were to become crucial. The targets are shown below in order of reducing frequency:

- Language development and bilingualism: these included the language across the curriculum and the use of all the pupils' languages in and for learning.
- Parental involvement: this covered the development of multi-lingual communications with parents, parent–teacher partnerships in the education of the child in the school and the home, and parental contributions to the assessment of pupils, which was at times carried out bilingually.
- Resources: the work dealt with bias and stereotyping in materials by either removing it or, more often, by developing the pupils' ability to recognize and deal with it.
- Subject-specific: schools developed their curriculum schemes, including teaching methods, in the core and some foundation subjects of the National Curriculum, in the pastoral curriculum and also in cross-curricular issues.
- Policy development: this work focused on the production of anti-racist policies and on whole-school policies in order better to meet the specific needs of pupils.

- Staffing: this involved work on the recruitment and development opportunities for ethnic minority staff.

The approach was well resourced through training grants so that schools were not only able to access courses but also able to release teachers to carry out developmental work and to learn from each other through direct observation of other teachers' classes (sometimes in other schools). The original approach had envisaged the provision of courses for one governor per school to help governing bodies to carry out their own responsibilities. The regulations governing grants at the time (1987) did not permit this feature to proceed; however most schools reported their developments and evaluations to their governing bodies. LEA advisers also monitored the work carried out in schools.

The programmers success was considerable despite the enforced omission of the governor training component and the somewhat subjective means of judging pupil achievement. The former was corrected soon after and is dealt with below in our discussion of training for governing bodies (GT), while the latter is increasingly driven by the assessment arrangements of the National Curriculum, the requirement to publish the assessment outcomes for schools and the development of records of achievement which include a wider concept of achievement than do examinations or standardized assessment tasks. The strength of the approach lies in:

- the location of responsibilities in a way which fits within the present context;
- the scope for LEAs to provide systematic support;
- the model used to manage change in schools.

Clearly, there is much within this approach that can survive the current changes. Equally clearly, the LEA INSET described is now outside the new regulations for the use of Section 11 funding and will have to be provided through mainstream funded advisory staff.

Quality development in schools

Quality Development (QD) as a distinctive feature of policy and practice within the LEA was a feature of the approach described above and also of an approach developed in our colleges almost simultaneously. The two approaches had much in common although the focus on evaluation was sharper in QD. Two shared key elements were:

- the use of evaluation as a tool and vehicle for change, with the responsibility located within schools or colleges, while LEA provided the framework, resource, support and moderation;
- the purpose of evaluation was seen to be the improvement of practice, with the schools or colleges seen as being responsible for the practice while using LEA support to enhance it.

The QD approach was launched in the schools sector in 1990, when the nature of recent educational and legislative changes was clearer. The lead adviser was Elizabeth Burridge, who had developed the approach with colleges. The similarity between MC and QD has been one of the reasons that has led to a high level of involvement in QD for one of the authors (Deshpande). QD has three specific aims:

- to improve learning and teaching;
- to fulfil accountability requirements;
- to support curriculum research and development.

QD is most effective when it enables the identification of a 'quality gap' and helps the development of measures which close such a gap. The seven stages of a Quality Development Action Plan can be described as follows:

1 audit, stocktaking, or 'Where are we now?'
2 objective setting, or 'Where do we want to get to?'
3 setting priority targets, or 'What do we need to focus on?'
4 identifying tasks, roles and responsibilities and progress checks, or 'How do we get there?'
5 carrying out the development, or 'Getting there'
6 progress review, formative evaluation, or 'How are we doing?'
7 success checks, summative evaluation, or 'How have we done?'

Such an action plan is intended to be cyclic and can be applied to any aspect of education. The features which impact on achievement identified in MC can utilize the process to produce focused action at any level which can be located within the classroom, the school as a whole or the school within the community. QD, like MC, seeks to involve all the stakeholders in education to play a part in the process. QD differs from MC in that MC set specific aims while QD sets much more general aims. In both approaches it is the schools that set their objectives. It would, however, be wrong to see QD as a value-free process. Its aims, although stated differently, include those of MC.

QD has been piloted with 19 schools which represent a cross-section of the schools in the City. It has been externally evaluated by the University of Birmingham and has been found to be a resounding success. One hundred and fifty additional schools are now at differing stages in the implementation of the approach.

The delivery of QD uses a strategy that is very similar to that used for MC. The main differences are that the training for the school's lead facilitator, called the QD Co-ordinator, is delivered through an Advanced Certificate in Education course, jointly designed and delivered by the LEA and the University of Birmingham, and that the MC support teachers are replaced by the LEA advisers and University tutors to provide support for one year. Of course, the LEA adviser role in supporting schools in QD continues beyond the year.

The process model offered by QD is very powerful, although it can only deliver an education for equality if the school uses it to focus on issues of equality. The support role of the LEA is as important in ensuring that the meaning invested in the term 'Quality' includes 'race' and gender equality. There is evidence available from the 19-school pilot which suggests that schools, advisers and University tutors have interpreted 'Quality' in this way.

At present the approaches within QD and CT are certainly compatible and work has started to make the relationship even more overt. The following section describes the issues that have been dealt with in our governor training programmes.

Training for governing bodies

As stated earlier, the 1986 (No. 2) Act and the Education Reform Act 1988 increased the power and responsibilities of governing bodies. Governing bodies now manage school budgets, set policies and priorities, appoint and dismiss staff, can propose to opt out of local authority control and decide how school buildings may be used after school hours. With this amount of power devolved to governing bodies it is no wonder that LEAs are apprehensive about their future role in relation to managing and supporting schools.

Governing bodies are made up of parent governors who are elected by the parents of pupils on the school roll, teacher governors, also elected by teaching staff, LEA governors who are nominated by the political parties depending on local council policy, and co-opted governors, who are co-opted by the rest of the governors to ensure that there is a balance in terms of race, gender and representation from industry. The headteacher can choose to be *ex officio* or a voting member of the governing body.

The issue of balance has to be addressed almost at every opportunity through election literature, training courses and essential reading for governors. Governing bodies were formed to make education accountable and to give the stakeholders a voice in decision-making. Unless the governing bodies reflect the local and wider community the interests of all children will not be central to policy-making.

The onslaught of legislative reforms since the mid-1980s has left little time for evaluating the effects of the changes. This is particularly true for governors, who have found it difficult to digest information and fully understand their roles and responsibilities. In Birmingham a training needs analysis was carried out as part of the initial induction course for all governors to establish the knowledge base and develop a training programme based on governors' perceived needs. As part of the programme a series of conferences on 'Race Equality – a positive approach to governing schools' were offered. The Conferences aimed to: highlight areas of the Education Reform Act that have special implications for racial equality; assist governors to formulate effective equal opportunities policies; and identify specific issues relating to equal opportunities that can be studied in depth at later meetings. All the conferences were oversubscribed and the participants set their own developmental programme of looking at specific issues such as bilingualism, racial harassment, community involvement, and religious education and collective worship. The evaluation sheets confirmed verbal feedback that governors from all parts of Birmingham had found these conferences invaluable not only because the focus was on helping children achieve their potential but also because governors felt that they could do something to meet the specific needs of all children in their own schools.

One of the major problems for governors is that of communication. Their general complaint is that they suffer from information overload: they do not always have the time to read every circular and urgent letter which arrives from the DFE or the LEA. On the other hand, there is lack of information from the school. Headteachers' reports are not always sent out in advance and do not often address curriculum and management issues. Governors may not even know if they have any visiting or support staff in the school as this is often not deemed to be necessary information for governors.

Most of these situations can be avoided by ensuring that the governing body shares the workload by setting up a committee structure. All documents are disseminated according to governors' interests, and at full governing body meetings the appropriate person gives a digest of documents with points for action. Headteachers' reports should be about progress on school development planning, implementation of school policies, personnel issues and budget matters as well as good practice from particular pupils and staff.

Most headteachers communicate with parents through termly or monthly newsletters. Governors need to be part of this communication process so that accountability to parents is a constant and not an annual feature of the governors' work.

This should in principle highlight the need for being aware of appropriate language and languages which would enable parents from different backgrounds to become better informed about their children's schooling.

Staff are the most costly resource of any school. Much of the research on effectiveness of schools has mentioned well-qualified and motivated staff as an essential feature. Governors of delegated schools are responsible for appointing all staff with the agreement of the LEA. Many governors feel completely inadequate in taking part in this process as they feel that they are unable to judge 'professionals'. Training governors in the process of recruitment and selection and following their progress in carrying out the task in their school, has been a wonderful experience. Without exception they have performed as well as or better than many of the professionals and have raised objections when any of the panel have asked discriminatory questions. Our recruitment and selection training programmes highlight areas of discrimination and explain the various pieces of legislation, such as the Race Relations Act 1976 and the Sex Discrimination Act 1975, of which governors need to be aware.

Individual governors do not have any power to make decisions, except for the chair and then only in two instances when authorized by the whole governing body for a specific reason or when the safety of the school is threatened. The philosophy behind the 1986 No. 2 Act was largely concerned with democratizing decision-making in schools and colleges. The 1988 Act extended this by making accountable education which uses public money, by introducing open enrolment, grant-maintained schools, city technology colleges and making possible a return to a selective system of education. The Schools Act 1992 further developed this in offering more choice for parents and accountability by introducing the Parents' Charter, league tables, the publication of examination results and a different way of inspecting schools. These changes, momentous in themselves, have overwhelmed everyone involved in education, from pupils to LEA officers. While teachers have been busy trying to implement the National Curriculum and administer Standard Assessment Tasks (SATs) governors have been getting to grips with their roles and responsibilities, and parents have been finding out what new educational terms mean. LEA personnel have been trying to make sense of the latest circulars from the DFE. Equal opportunities issues have been put on the back burner.

Individual LEAs, schools and organizations are still carrying on heroically but, apart from the continuous Section 11 funding, the impetus for ensuring equality is left to the individual or the individual organization.

Governing bodies of all county and maintained schools started their new term of office in September 1988. Soon after this the

DES issued a press release and highlighted the need for more governors from ethnic minority groups/communities.

The now abolished Inner London Education Authority (ILEA) also carried out surveys, and established the fact that ethnic minority governors were underrepresented on governing bodies. The National Consumer Council, Community Development Foundation and Action for Governors' Information and Training (AGIT) carried out a survey of LEAs which were members of AGIT (60 at the time), to find out what LEAs were doing to (a) recruit more governors from ethnic minority communities and (b) support existing ones. Half of the surveyed authorities responded.

The findings were predictable. Ethnic minority governors were underrepresented in all of the authorities, but most of them were taking some steps to recruit more. Very few authorities were monitoring governing bodies and fewer still had any support groups or offered special training for their ethnic minority governors. The survey findings and recommendations were published in a report, *Minority Ethnic Communities and School Governing Bodies*, in October 1990.

Governing bodies have had to grow up very quickly; some have achieved a degree of maturity, while others still have teething problems. But as governors become established in their new role, assuming that role does not change again, their participation in the organization and management of schools will grow and become more sophisticated. This will, with appropriate training and support, develop greater awareness of social justice and equality.

To train this army of 300,000 governors, the DES set up an Education Support Grant, which LEAs were invited to bid for. The criteria for funding did not include ethnic minority governors or the need to monitor governing bodies. People who were appointed to take responsibility for governor training, known as governor training co-ordinators, came from varying backgrounds with varying understandings of equal opportunities issues.

HMI survey reports of governor training in 1988/89 and 1990/91 did not include equal opportunities training as a heading but did comment on the lack of ethnic minority governors. The NFER Survey Report 1991 also confirmed this.

While it would be idealistic to hope for a fairer representation of ethnic minority governors on governing bodies, the reality is that it is likely to take some time and a great deal of effort on the part of those who recruit governors, namely schools, voluntary-aided schools organizations, governing bodies, voluntary organizations and local authorities.

Governors can ask for a breakdown by 'race' and gender of examination entries and results; the assessment of pupils to identify those who may have learning needs as opposed to language development needs; which groups of children get excluded and for what reasons. The recent national interest in exclusions has highlighted once again the reoccurring issue of black children being excluded proportionally more than their white counterparts. Effective training and support can assist governors to become more knowledgeable about procedures for conducting exclusion meetings and avoid discriminating practices.

Governing bodies are largely made up of volunteers who for one reason or another want to help children and schools to be more effective. In democratizing educational decision-making there has been conflict, mainly between headteachers and governors. Autocratic headteachers have found it difficult to share power with governors who have either become disillusioned and resigned or caused conflict which has led to situations where the LEA has had to step in to mediate. The famous Stratford School case of 1992 which involved the headteacher and the chair of governors highlighted yet another dimension of this problem for grant-maintained schools.

Governors and headteachers need to work together, to enhance the educational opportunities for all the children in their care. These educational opportunities will only be enhanced if the governing body is aware of equal opportunities issues and ensures their implementation at all levels through school development planning. Pupils, parents, staff and governors all have to 'own' the school and its policies and work together to achieve these goals, otherwise equal opportunities policies will remain policies without action.

Governing bodies must hold an annual general meeting and publish an annual report for parents to inform them of examination results, budget management and school development plan targets. They need to ensure that the annual general meeting is held at a time which will allow all parents to attend, pick suitable venues for easy access. They should also examine the appropriateness of language(s) used for the Report.

Governing bodies are there to ensure that all children receive an effective education and are given equal chance to achieve through appropriate policies on staffing, budgeting, adequate and relevant resources and monitoring of the school development plan.

All these tools for management must ensure that the specific needs of black and ethnic minority children and girls are taken into account; for example, in school development plans areas for development should address specific implications for ethnic minority pupils and girls.

Index

MAKING SENSE OF TEACHING

Sally Brown and Donald McIntyre

This book helps us to understand better the nature of teaching in schools and, in particular, to understand teaching from the perspective of the people doing it: the teachers. The authors seek to gain access to teachers' professional craft knowledge and to facilitate teachers' own articulation of the ordinary, everyday teaching which they do routinely and spontaneously in classrooms. Their emphasis throughout is on investigating 'good teaching', on what goes well in the classroom. They are also concerned to identify how an understanding of the professional craft knowledge of teachers is particularly important for, and applicable to, the preservice and inservice training of teachers, effective curriculum innovation, and teacher appraisal. They help us to make sense of what goes on in good teaching, and draw out the significant implications for policy and practice.

Contents

Making sense of teaching: a priority for theory, policy and practice – Identifying 'good teaching' – How do teachers talk about their good teaching? – Generalizations across teachers: goals and actions – The conditions of teaching and a theoretical framework – The routines teachers use to achieve their goals – Making sense of teaching: conclusions and implications – References – Index.

144pp   0 335 15795 5 (Paperback)   0 335 15796 3 (Hardback)

CRITICAL FEMINISM
ARGUMENT IN THE DISCIPLINES
Kate Campbell (ed.)

Academic feminism can be too academic, and not a critical matter. Hence the insistence: *critical* feminism. The chapters of this book formally consider and informally demonstrate some of the differences that feminism makes in various academic disciplines and their surrounds: psychology, art, art history, history, social work and literary criticism. The closer focus of the chapters from literary critics balances the broad scope of others, disclosing particular issues and stances immediately engaging feminists. All in all the writers display the wide variety of approaches and assumptions that make feminism's identity elusive. In this they present a handbook for the uncertain, a field of contention for the initiated: an open house.

Particular attention is given to the relationships between:

- feminism and socialism
- feminism and deconstruction
- men and feminism
- academic discourse and wider cultural values
- theory and practice.

Contents

Introduction: matters of theory and practice, or, we'll be coming out the harbour – A lop-sided view: feminist history or the history of women? – Feminism and academic psychology: towards a psychology of women? – More than a method: feminist social work – Thrown together: Olive Schreiner, writing and politics – Feminism, class and literary criticism – Fellow-travelling with feminist criticism – Mary Kelly and Griselda Pollock in conversation – Index.

Contributors

Carolyn Burdett, Kate Campbell, Lena Dominelli, John Goode, Margaret Iversen, Mary Kelly, Paula Nicolson, Griselda Pollock, Rick Rylance, Deborah Thom.

240pp   0 335 09757 X (Paperback)

READING AGAINST RACISM

Emrys Evans (ed.)

Reading Against Racism addresses the reading and teaching of literature and its relationship to differences of race and culture in English-speaking countries. It assumes that literature in English should be drawn from different cultures and countries in order to foster in readers self-knowledge and awareness of cultural diversity. Practically oriented, it recommends and discusses the classroom use of novels, poems and plays written in the Indian subcontinent, South Africa, the Caribbean, the USA and other countries. Drawing upon a number of different traditions, and coming from a number of different countries and backgrounds, the contributors show how reading literature can be a basic plank in anti-racist education. As Anthony Adams writes in his introduction: 'In its consistent advocacy of a positive approach to the challenge of anti-racist education and its celebration of the role of literature in this context, it breaks new ground in its thinking and provides a beginning for committed classroom work.'

Contents

Contributors

Napheas Akhter, Rudine Sims Bishop, Emrys Evans, Jim Kable, Shahana Mirza, Beverley Naidoo, Denise Newfield, Sibani Raychaudhuri, Lena Strang.

176pp   0 335 09544 5 (Paperback)

DATE DUE

AUG 0 1 1999			
OCT 2 0 2000			
NOV 1 8 2014			
GAYLORD			PRINTED IN U.S.A.